Christina Sheffield

High Yields *in* High Heels

WOMEN ROCKING THE STOCK MARKET

Christina Sheffield

High Yields *in* High Heels

First Edition

WOMEN ROCKING THE STOCK MARKET

Law of Attraction Calendar LLC

High Yields in High Heels:
Women Rocking the Stock Market

Written by Christina Sheffield

Publisher Law of Attraction Calendar LLC

Copyright © 2024 Law of Attraction Calendar LLC

Design by Sassy Design Studio

Table of Contents

Part I

Investing Basics:

Building Your Financial Fortress Without the Facepalms

Part II

Crafting Your Investment Masterplan:

Or, How to Stop Wingin' It and Start Stacking Cash

Part III
Making Money Moves

Foreword

For far too long, the stubborn notion that women don't belong in finance and that men are naturally better at it has stuck around — much like those old myths about using only 10% of our brains or that a mother bird will reject her baby if you touch it with bare hands. Spoiler alert: they're all nonsense! This book is here to bust those outdated beliefs and show how a simple shift in mindset can unlock financial success for anyone, regardless of gender.

Imagine a world where financial smarts aren't determined by chromosomes but by competence and creativity. Research shows that diverse teams, including those led by women, often achieve better financial outcomes. Why? Because mixing perspectives is like mixing cocktails — it's always better with variety! Different viewpoints lead to better decisions, more innovation, and, ultimately, more money in everyone's pockets. In fact, the 2019 analysis by McKinsey & Company found that companies with more women on their executive teams are 25% more likely to be profitable. Plus, Fidelity Investments says women investors tend to outperform men by 0.4% annually, thanks to their patient and consistent strategies.

Women in finance have been breaking barriers and showing they mean business. Trailblazers like Mellody Hobson of Ariel Investments and Abigail Johnson of Fidelity Investments have proven that women can lead financial powerhouses and deliver great results. According to Catalyst's 2007 study "The Bottom Line: Corporate Performance and Women's Representation on Boards," companies with more women on their boards significantly outperform those with the least women. They achieve 53% higher return on equity, 42% higher return on sales, and a remarkable 66% higher return on invested capital. These impressive statistics underscore the substantial financial benefits of gender diversity in

corporate leadership, proving that having more women on boards isn't just fair —
it's smart business.

Recognizing the power of smart investments, this book serves as your ultimate
guide to financial freedom through the thrilling world of stocks. Think of it as
your financial GPS, ready to lead you to success — because who starts a road trip
without a map? With practical, no-nonsense steps, I'll show you how to cruise
through the sometimes bumpy roads of investing without blowing a tire! Given
that the stock market has historically returned an average of 10% annually,
according to JP Morgan, it's clear that investing wisely can yield significant
rewards. Many millionaires and billionaires, including legends like Warren Buffett,
have made their fortunes through smart investments. In fact, 90% of millionaires in
the U.S. invest in stocks, proving the stock market's serious wealth-building
power.

Whether you're just dipping your toes into the finance pool or already plotting
your way to money mogul status, this book is your new best friend — armed with
all the confidence-boosting and success-making tools you need to shine!

So, let's move beyond those tired stereotypes. Let's break free from outdated
thinking and stride confidently into a future where everyone can thrive in finance.
After all, money doesn't care about your gender — so why should we? Buckle up,
because your journey to financial empowerment starts here, and trust me, it's going
to be a fun ride!

Introduction

If you've ever felt like your life was one endless loop of packed lunches, mortgage payments, and dodging the vacuum cleaner robot, welcome to the club! My life was the epitome of average — a loving spouse, a couple of energetic kids, and two dogs who thought chasing their own tails was the pinnacle of daily excitement. We dove headfirst into the American Dream with student debt heavier than my Mom's cheesecake and credit card bills that had us gasping for air like we were running a marathon with cement shoes. Yet, through the chaos and financial juggling, we held onto the hope that one day we'd trade those bills for beach cocktails and carefree afternoons. We heard about people making a fortune in the stock market, turning their investments into substantial wealth, and it got us thinking about our own financial future. The idea of growing our money beyond just paying off debt started to take root.

I craved more than just making ends meet. My dreams aimed higher — like actually affording that fancy imported cheese at the supermarket and not just the rubbery stuff called "cheddar." But seriously, I wanted my kids to bask in the wonder and joy of childhood, from magical trips to the theme park to all the sprinkles on their ice cream cones. Flash to the moment when my youngest developed an enchanting obsession with Mickey Mouse. A whimsical weekend at the amusement park? Dream on.

Financing such a trip wasn't an option. As a former bank employee, I saw firsthand how those menacing interest rates could strangle dreams faster than a pair of too-tight jeans on Thanksgiving. Ironically, despite money being life's mantra at the bank, none of us were swimming in it.

That's when I decided to take matters into my own hands. I couldn't change the beginning, but I could start from here and create a fantastic ending! Countless books later (surely enough to fill a small library or at least a decently large bathroom), I stumbled upon the golden goose: investing. While I understood the basics — buy low, sell high — I needed to dig deeper to avoid gambling away those precious pennies.

Here's where the magic happens! In this book, I'll share my journey from clueless to competent, laying out the exact steps I took to identify exceptional companies worth your hard-earned money. And guess what? If I can do it, so can you.

PART I

Investing Basics:
Building Your Financial Fortress Without the Facepalms

Chapter 1

Breaking Down Barriers Without Breaking a Nail

Alright, let me spill the beans. I grew up with parents who were the absolute epitome of the 9-to-5 life. They were like walking motivational posters for phrases such as "luck, connections, and natural talent create wealth," "money is the root of all evil," and, my personal favorite, "money doesn't grow on trees." Naturally, I swallowed these gems whole, thinking they were the golden rules of life.

Family gatherings were like support groups for penny-pinchers. And friends? They whispered about money as if it was the world's best-kept secret. When funds were low, we went full detective mode, counting pennies like we were Indiana Jones searching for treasures. Couch cushions got a pat down for loose change.

Turning those penny-pinching, scarcity-driven beliefs on their head felt like trading the comfort of your favorite, albeit washed-out, sweater for a Chanel blazer that I wasn't sure was meant for me. Suddenly, I had to walk around with a brand-new "can-do" attitude, which felt like attempting to juggle flaming torches while riding a unicycle. It was thrilling, a bit wobbly, and required a whole new level of balance and confidence I wasn't sure I had. Here is how you can achieve this as well:

Unleashing Your Inner Wonder Woman: Mindset Shifts for Supercharged Success

Visualize Success: Take a few minutes daily to imagine your success. Create a vision board every year and hang it where you spend most of your time. Define how you want your year to look and where you want to be in life. Use drawing, painting, or collaging to create visual representations of your goals. It's like being the star of your own epic movie, with a montage of you nailing your goals. Feel the excitement, the triumphs, and the positive impact on your life. This mental movie will keep your motivation strong and laser-focused on success.

For example, imagine being so wealthy that you can buy all the tickets for that long-overdue girls' vacation. Visualize you and your best friends sipping cocktails on a beach, enjoying fun boat rides, and watching dolphins dance in the waves. Add these pictures to your vision board and, every time you look at it, think about the laughter, the shared memories, and the sheer joy of having a great time together. This daily visualization will keep your spirits high and your goals in sight, making each step toward financial freedom feel like a celebrated scene in your personal success story.

Set Clear, Achievable Goals: Think of your goals as a giant, unwieldy chocolate cake. Instead of attempting to eat the whole thing in one go (cue tummy ache), cut it into small, delicious slices. Each slice is a manageable task. Plus, who doesn't love bite-sized pieces? Celebrate every little victory with a sprinkle of confetti (or maybe just an extra indulgent cup of coffee).

Here's a great example: The goal is to run a marathon.
Slice 1: Buy running shoes
Slice 2: Start with a 1-mile walk, increasing your speed by a little each day
Slice 3: By week 2, start with a 1-mile run
Slice 4: Increase distance by half a mile each week
Slice 5: Register and run in a local 5K race as a milestone
Slice 6: Repeat step 4 until you can join a 10K race as a milestone
Slice 7: Keep increasing the distance by half a mile each week until you reach the 26.2 mile mark (42 km)
Slice 8: Register, run, and celebrate your first marathon

Each step is manageable and celebratory. You'll reach your ultimate goal without feeling overwhelmed, and every achievement along the way gets you closer to that marathon finish line!

Or, since this is a book about money, if your ultimate goal is to save $5,000 this year, break it down into smaller, achievable goals like saving $100 a week. Each week, as you hit that target, treat yourself to a small reward—like an at-home spa day, a fancy latte, or a new book to keep your mind sharp. By focusing on these smaller goals, you'll stay motivated and make steady progress toward the big prize.

Cultivate Positive Self-Talk: Next, you need to become your own cheerleader. Swap those negative thoughts for positive affirmations. Imagine if your brain was a garden. Negative self-talk is like pesky weeds, while positive affirmations are the beautiful flowers you're planting.

Negative Self-Talk: "I can't do this." Positive Self-Talk: "This is challenging, but I can learn and improve with practice."
Negative Self-Talk: "I always fail." Positive Self-Talk: "Every failure is a learning opportunity. I am getting closer to my goal."
Negative Self-Talk: "I'm not good enough." Positive Self-Talk: "I have unique strengths and abilities that I can develop further."

Practice Gratitude: Ladies, it's time to start counting your blessings like you count your shoes! Shifting your focus from what's missing to what you have can work wonders for your mindset. Keeping a gratitude journal and writing down a few things you're grateful for each day is like giving yourself a daily pep talk with the Universe. Research shows that practicing gratitude can lead to a happier, healthier life. Studies have found that regularly acknowledging what you're grateful for can improve emotional well-being, reduce stress, and even enhance physical health. Based on a study featured in the Journal of Personality and Social Psychology, people who kept gratitude journals reported fewer symptoms of illness, felt better about their lives, and were more optimistic about the future. Think of it as a mini-celebration of the good things in your life. Who knew writing "I'm thankful for coffee and comfy leggings" could be so life-changing? Plus, it's a fabulous way to end the day on a positive note, making you feel more connected and content. So go ahead, grab that journal, and start counting your blessings – your inner glow will thank you!

Embrace Failure as a Learning Opportunity: Fear of failure? Pfft, that's so last season! Think of every mistake as a fabulous detour on your path to success. Each setback is like a personal trainer for your brain, helping you get stronger and smarter. Instead of seeing failure as a dead-end, view it as a learning curve. When life hands you lemons, analyze them, strategize their perfect squeeze, and move ahead with zest! Reflect on what went wrong and what could have been done differently. Use these insights to develop a concrete action plan for improvement. Celebrate small wins along the way to keep motivated. Take inspiration from J.K. Rowling, who faced numerous rejections from publishers before finding success with the Harry Potter series. She used each rejection as motivation to improve and persevere, eventually creating a beloved literary empire. Embrace failure, learn from it, and let it be the stepping stone to your fabulous, unstoppable success!

Surround Yourself with Positivity: Ever heard the saying, "You're the result of the five closest people in your circle?" Well, if your squad is all about positivity, you're golden! Beyond just the financially savvy BFFs, make sure your inner circle includes upbeat, motivating individuals. Sprinkle in some positive media, and uplifting activities, and you'll be the positive powerhouse of the group.

Research supports the idea that the people and media we surround ourselves with have a significant impact on our mindset and overall well-being. A study published in the Journal of Social and Personal Relationships found that positive social interactions can increase life satisfaction and reduce stress. Another study in the Journal of Psychological Science revealed that emotions can be contagious; being around positive people can boost your own mood and outlook.

Additionally, consuming positive media content has been shown to improve mood and foster a sense of well-being, according to research published in the Journal of Communication. So, keep your circle and your media diet full of positivity – it's scientifically proven to make you shine!

Stay Informed and Educated: Get your knowledge game on! Staying informed and educated is your ticket to success. In today's fast-paced world, keeping up with trends and information is crucial. Whether it's devouring insightful books, attending snazzy seminars, or binge-watching expert webinars, keeping that brilliant brain of yours well-fed is essential. Dive into industry journals, subscribe to newsletters, and follow thought leaders on social media to stay ahead of the curve. Enroll in online courses to acquire new skills or deepen your expertise. Think of yourself as the chic librarian of the digital age, with a well-organized collection of knowledge at your fingertips, ready to pull out the right facts and strategies when needed. Knowledge is not just power; it's your secret weapon in standing out and staying relevant. So, grab those reading glasses, fire up those webinars, and immerse yourself in learning – your future self will thank you for being so fabulously well-informed and ahead of the game!

Practice Self-Care: A winning mindset isn't just about brainpower; it's about treating yourself like the queen you are. Embracing self-care is key to achieving this regal state. Regular exercise, a nutritious diet, and beauty sleep are your new besties, essential for maintaining your energy and focus. Exercise not only keeps you fit but also releases endorphins, the feel-good hormones that boost your mood and productivity. Eating a balanced diet rich in vitamins and minerals fuels your body and brain, giving you the stamina to tackle challenges head-on. Beauty sleep is non-negotiable; it's when your body repairs itself and your mind processes the day's events, leaving you refreshed and ready to conquer the next day. Incorporate some meditation or yoga into your routine to cultivate inner peace and mindfulness. These practices help lower stress, improve focus, and make you feel better overall. Picture yourself as the zen master of productivity, effortlessly balancing work and relaxation. Remember, a healthy mind and body are the ultimate power duo. Prioritizing self-care means you're investing in your most valuable asset: yourself. So, go ahead, indulge in that bubble bath, enjoy your favorite healthy snack, and get those extra hours of sleep.

Develop Resilience: Think of resilience as your inner Wonder Woman, ready to tackle any challenge that comes your way. Strengthening this superpower involves cultivating a positive outlook, staying adaptable, and always keeping your long-term vision in sight. Research from the American Psychological Association suggests that resilience is not an innate trait but a set of behaviors, thoughts, and actions that can be learned and developed by anyone.

To develop your own resilience, start by reframing setbacks as opportunities for growth. Embrace change and be flexible in your approach, recognizing that sometimes detours can lead to the most scenic routes. Keep your eye on the prize, reminding yourself of your long-term goals and why they matter to you. Practice self-compassion during tough times, and don't hesitate to reach out to friends, family, or mentors for support. Resilience is similar to a muscle; the more you exercise it, the stronger it becomes. So, when life presents challenges, channel your inner Wonder Woman, high-kick your way through the challenges, and emerge stronger and more determined. You've got this!

Seek Mentorship and Guidance: Find a fabulous mentor who's already where you want to be! Their advice is like having a VIP pass to the success concert. A great mentor can provide invaluable insights, help you navigate challenges, and offer guidance based on their own experiences. Research from the Harvard Business Review shows that professionals with mentors are more likely to get promoted and experience greater career satisfaction. For example, Sheryl Sandberg, COO of Facebook, attributes much of her success to the mentorship she received from leaders like Larry Summers. Their guidance helped her develop the skills and confidence needed to excel in her career.

When seeking a mentor, look for someone whose career path aligns with your goals and who exemplifies the qualities you admire. Whether it's in your current career, the stock market, or any other goals you have in life, don't be shy—reach out, express your admiration for their work, and ask if they'd be willing to share their journey and offer advice. Prepare thoughtful questions, actively listen, and apply their wisdom to your own path. Remember, a mentor's journey can illuminate your own, providing a roadmap to success. It's like having a personal Yoda, minus the green skin—someone who can see your potential, challenge you to grow, and cheer you on every step of the way.

Celebrate Small Wins: Don't wait for the big finish to pop the champagne—every victory, no matter how small, deserves its moment in the spotlight. Celebrating small wins is essential for maintaining motivation and building momentum toward larger goals. Research from Harvard Business School highlights the importance of recognizing small achievements, showing that frequent celebrations of progress can significantly boost happiness and productivity. For example, think of the satisfaction of finally organizing your closet. That small triumph not only makes your space more functional but also gives you a sense of accomplishment and control. Similarly, nailing that presentation at work is a confidence booster that reinforces your capabilities and prepares you for bigger challenges.

To maximize the benefits of celebrating small wins, establish a habit of acknowledging your progress regularly. Keep a journal to track daily or weekly achievements, no matter how minor they may seem. Reward yourself in meaningful ways, such as treating yourself to your favorite coffee, taking a relaxing bath, or enjoying a night out with friends. These celebrations create a positive feedback loop, encouraging you to keep pushing forward. Remember, each small win is a step toward your ultimate goals, and taking the time to celebrate them can keep you pumped and ready for more. So, go ahead and toast to your successes, both big and small—your journey to greatness is made up of these wonderful, celebratory moments!

You achieve wealth in your mind long before you attain it in your assets. By consistently sprinkling these fabulous strategies into your daily routine, you're turning your life into a dynamic engine of personal growth and success. Picture yourself not just chasing achievements but enjoying every twist and turn along the way, making each step a cherished part of your story. With a blend of gratitude, self-care, and celebrating small wins, you're not just reaching for the stars; you're loving the climb, too. Mentorship and continuous learning become your secret weapons, giving you the edge to navigate life's challenges with flair. By integrating these practices, you're not just crafting a life of success but one that's deeply fulfilling and ever-evolving, like a fabulous adventure where you're the star of the show.

Smashing the Myths About Women and Investing

Women Lack Financial Knowledge: The misconception that women lack financial knowledge is a myth that has been debunked by numerous studies over the years. The research provided at the beginning of this book is just some of the many studies that support this. Women not only have substantial financial acumen but also tend to be more diligent in seeking out information and advice before making investment decisions. This careful, research-oriented approach often leads to more informed and potentially more successful financial outcomes. Therefore, the idea that women lack financial knowledge is not only outdated but also incorrect, as women continue to demonstrate their competence and expertise in managing finances and investments effectively.

Women Don't Invest: The assumption that women don't participate in the investment world as actively as men is outdated and has been challenged by recent research. A study conducted by Fidelity Investments in 2021 found that two-thirds of women are now actively investing their savings, which marks a significant increase from previous years. This surge in female participation in the investment world is not just a trend but a growing movement. Women are taking charge of their financial futures, armed with research, resources, and a keen interest in growing their wealth. Far from being passive players, women are now starring as the lead roles in their financial journeys, bringing a fresh perspective and dynamic approach to the investment landscape. Move over, Wall Street wolves—there's a new pack in town, and they're here to take the investment world by storm!

Women's Investments Are Less Successful: There's a false impression that women's investment portfolios underperform. Well, guess what? Research shows that women often have equal or even better investment outcomes, thanks to their disciplined and steady approach. Besides the Fidelity study I mentioned earlier, the Warwick Business School revealed in 2018 that women's portfolios performed better than men's over a three-year period, with women achieving returns of 1.8% higher on average. This isn't just a happy accident; it's a testament to the power of thoughtful, research-driven investing. Women tend to be more patient and risk-averse, avoiding the trap of frequent trading and impulsive decisions that can erode returns. So, let's rewrite the script: women are not just keeping up; they're leading the way in the investment world. Now that's a plot twist worthy of the big screen!

Women Don't Have Time for Investing: Contrary to popular belief, women actually have a hidden superpower. Not only can they juggle more tasks than a circus performer on caffeine, but they've also got more brain cells than men! That's right, more brain cells – like a built-in Wi-Fi system that's always connected.

With this extra mental bandwidth, women can process information faster and handle ten things at once, all while sipping a latte and watching the newest season of their favorite series. So, managing investments? Piece of cake! Women effectively use technology to stay informed, making time management look like a breeze.

Let's face it: if you can manage a household, a career, a social life, and binge-watch Netflix all at once, keeping an eye on your investments is just another item on your yes-I-can-do-it list.

Chapter 2

Budgeting for Babes: Finding Money to Invest

Before diving into the exciting world of investing, you need to know where you stand financially. Think of it as a treasure hunt, where the prize is your financial freedom. By understanding your income, expenses, net worth, and debts, you can uncover hidden funds to invest. This quick financial snapshot is the beginning of your journey towards a prosperous future.

Financial Selfie: Snap Your Net Worth in High Definition

Now it's time to figure out your financial net worth—which is basically your financial selfie in high definition! Start by gathering all your assets. This includes cash, savings, investments, retirement accounts, real estate, and yes, even that fabulous designer handbag collection. Next, add up all these assets to get a total.

But we're not done yet. Now, it's time to tackle your liabilities. These are your debts, such as credit card balances, student loans, mortgages, and any other bills you owe. Subtract the total amount of your liabilities from your assets, and voilà! You have your net worth.

Think of it as a financial report card that gives you a snapshot of your overall financial health. It tells you how much you own versus how much you owe, helping you understand your financial position better. Whether your net worth is in the positive or negative, this number is your starting point. It's like knowing your exact position on the financial map, so you can plot your course to financial success.

To sum it up, defining your net worth is a powerful way to see the bigger picture of your finances. It's your personal balance sheet, showing where you stand financially and guiding you towards smarter financial decisions. So go ahead, crunch those numbers and embrace your status as a financial superstar!

To get a fun and clear snapshot of your financial standing, dive into this Net Worth Overview right here!

Net Worth Overview

Assets

Liquid Assets	Market Value
Checking Account	
Savings Account	
Cash	
Other:	
Investment Assets	
Retirement Account	
Stocks/Bond Inv.	
CDs	
Fixed Income	
Other:	
Personal Assets	
Personal Property	
Vehicles	
Collectibles	
Jewelry	
Other:	
Real Estate	
Personal Residence	
Rental Properties	
Other:	
Other Assets	
Life Ins. Cash Value	
Other:	
Business Interests	
Ownership Stakes	
Other:	
Total Assets	

Liabilities

Short-Term Liabilities	Market Value
Credit Card Debt	
Personal Loans	
Taxes Owed	
Other:	
Long-Term Liabilities	
Mortgage	
Student Loans	
Auto Loans	
Other:	
Total Liabilities	

Net Worth

Total Assets	
- Total Liabilities	
Total Net Worth	

Notes

Treasure Hunt: Discovering Hidden Wealth in Your Budget

It's time to channel your inner financial diva and give your wallet a fabulous makeover! First, let's take a good, hard look at your financial selfie that you took earlier. Think of this as the wardrobe audit before a major shopping spree. Pull out all your receipts, bank statements, and credit card bills. Lay them out like you're about to Marie Kondo your closet. Let's figure out where your money is going — and if it's sparking joy or just burning holes in your wallet.

But we're not stopping there. To truly assess your financial situation, dive deeper by categorizing your expenses into must-haves (like housing, groceries, and utilities) and nice-to-haves (like that daily latte or those spontaneous online shopping sprees). Are you spending too much on things that don't bring long-term happiness or value? It's like discovering you've been hoarding clothes that still have tags on them. Time to declutter those unnecessary expenses!

Next, tally up your income. How much are you actually bringing in each month? Compare this with your expenses to see if you're living within your means or stretching your budget too thin. This step is crucial because it's the foundation for your financial goals. Think of it as knowing your exact clothing size before hitting the mall—no more squeezing into something that doesn't fit!

Let's talk debt and savings. How much do you owe, and what's the interest rate on those debts? How much do you have stashed away for a rainy day? Knowing these numbers helps you plan your next steps. It's like checking the weather before planning an outdoor event — essential for avoiding surprises. Analyze your spending habits. Are you impulse buying or planning each purchase? Recognizing these patterns can help you make more informed financial decisions.

So, grab a cup of your favorite tea, put on some empowering music, and dive into this financial makeover. By the end, you'll not only have a clearer picture of your financial health but also feel empowered to make savvy decisions that bring you closer to where you want to be financially.

Now that you've got a clear snapshot of your financial situation, it's time to take things to the next level with monthly budgeting. Budgeting is like the ultimate fashion plan for your finances—it ensures you're showing off the runway of life in style without tripping over unexpected expenses. By creating a budget (and sticking to it), you set the stage for achieving your financial goals, whether it's saving for that dream vacation, paying off debt, or investing in your future.

To get you started, here's a handy budget planner you can use to uncover all the hidden money traps and guide you on your path to financial success! It's all about turning your money woes into financial wows and steering your ship confidently toward the treasure chest of financial freedom.

Budget Planner

Total Income	Total Expenses	Ending Balance

Income	Amount
Total Income	

Notes

Expenses	Amount
Housing	
Utilities	
Food	
Debt	
Medical	
Insurance	
Donations	
Savings	
Personal	
Total Expenses	

Track your spending for a month and spot the unnecessaries. Every latte, every impulse buy, every tiny splurge—treat it like you're Sherlock Holmes on the trail of runaway cash. Once you know where every dollar is fleeing, you can start reining them in.

Start by recording every expense, no matter how small. Use a notebook, a budgeting app, or a spreadsheet to keep track of your daily spending. Each entry is a clue, bringing you closer to solving the mystery of where your money goes.

At the end of the month, sit down with your list and take a magnifying glass to your expenses. Are there any subscriptions you're not using? Perhaps a gym membership you forgot about or a streaming service you never watch? Those are your budget busters, and it's time to give them the boot!

Look at your weekly expenses. Are you dining out more often than necessary? Could you trim down your grocery bill by planning meals and avoiding food waste?

Spotting these patterns helps you identify where to cut back without sacrificing your lifestyle.

Create categories for your spending, such as food, entertainment, transportation, and personal care. This helps you see where your money is going and highlights areas where you might be overspending. Compare these categories to your income and see if any adjustments are needed.

Consider setting spending limits for each category. For instance, allocate a certain amount for dining out and stick to it. If you exceed the limit, it's a sign to cut back next month.

Once you've identified the unnecessary expenses, wave goodbye to what you don't need. Cancel those unused subscriptions, cut down on the daily coffee runs, and rethink that spontaneous shopping spree. More cash for what truly matters— like building your savings, paying off debt, or treating yourself to something special once in a while.

By tracking your spending diligently, you're not only uncovering the hidden money traps but also paving the way for smarter financial decisions. It's like putting on your detective hat and transforming your budget into a well-oiled machine.

Crush the Debt — It's a Drama Queen

Debt is the ultimate drama queen of finances. It's draining your wallet faster than a broken faucet thanks to interest and that sneaky beast called compound interest. Compound interest is like glitter — it sticks around and multiplies! Tackle your debt head-on by creating a payoff plan.

Alright, as an example, picture this: Let's say I did book that unforgettable theme park vacation with the family. Instead of a weekend, I decided to book it for a whole week because once I'm there I want to enjoy myself and not rush back to the airport right away. Flights, hotels, rental car, tickets, dining — the whole nine yards — racking up a cool $10,000 on my credit card. Why? Because someone somewhere said it's great to "build credit."

Now, here's where the fun begins. Let's add in a not-so-magical 20% APR (annual percentage rate) on that credit card. If I don't pay it off right away, compound interest starts working its mischievous tricks.

Compound interest in debt is like interest on steroids, but unfortunately, it's working against you. When you have debt, the interest you owe gets added to the principal, and in future periods, you owe interest on both the original amount and the accumulated interest. It's like a debt snowball rolling down a hill, picking up more and more debt as it goes. Instead of your money growing, your debt grows faster over time, making it harder to pay off. Picture it as your debt hitting the gym and getting supercharged gains, but not in a good way. It's your financial nightmare gaining momentum!

The Compound Interest Formula: $A = P(1 + r)^t$

Where:

- (A) = The amount of money accumulated after (t) years, including interest.
- (P) = The principal amount (the initial borrowed amount), which is \$10,000 in this case.
- (r) = Annual interest rate (decimal), so 20% becomes 0.20.
- (t) = The number of years.

Calculations

Year 1: $A = 10,000$ USD $(1+0.20)^1$
$A = 10,000$ USD $\times 1.20$
$A = 12,000.00$ USD

Year 2: $A = 10,000$ USD $(1+0.20)^2$
$A = 10,000$ USD $\times 1.44$
$A = 14,400.00$ USD

Year 3: $A = 10,000$ USD $(1+0.20)^3$
$A = 10,000$ USD $\times 1.728$
$A = 17,280.00$ USD

Year 4: $A = 10,000$ USD $(1+0.20)^4$
$A = 10,000$ USD $\times 2.0736$
$A = 20,736.00$ USD

Year 5: $A = 10,000$ USD $(1+0.20)^5$
$A = 10,000$ USD $\times 2.48832$
$A = 24,883.20$ USD

Year 6: $A = 10,000$ USD $(1+0.20)^6$
$A = 10,000$ USD $\times 2.985984$
$A = 29,859.84$ USD

Year 7: $A = 10,000$ USD $(1+0.20)^7$
$A = 10,000$ USD $\times 3.583181$
$A = 35,831.81$ USD

Year 8: $A = 10,000$ USD $(1+0.20)^8$
$A = 10,000$ USD $\times 4.299817$
$A = 42,998.17$ USD

Year 9: $A = 10,000$ USD $(1+0.20)^9$
$A = 10,000$ USD $\times 5.159780$
$A = 51,597.80$ USD

Year 10: $A = 10,000$ USD $(1+0.20)^{10}$
$A = 10,000$ USD $\times 6.191736$
$A = 61,917.36$ USD

Breaking It Down in Less Scary Terms:

Year 1: Your \$10,000 Theme park adventure swells to approximately \$12,000.
Year 2: Your debt grows to about \$14,400.
Year 3: The balance increases to roughly \$17,280.

Year 4: You'll owe about $20,736.

Year 5: Your once $10,000 trip is now a sizable $24,883.20.

Year 6: Your debt now stands at $29,859.84, nearly triple the original cost of your
trip.

Year 7: The balance continues to balloon to $35,831.81, making that vacation
seem like a distant, expensive memory.

Year 8: By now, the debt has increased to $42,998.17, turning your theme park
fun into a financial fright.

Year 9: The amount owed swells to $51,597.80, surpassing the cost of many new
cars.

Year 10: Take a deep breath; it's now an eye-popping $61,917.36!

So, unless the Mouse himself offers to pay off your debt, it's wise to tackle that
balance ASAP. Compound interest is magical if it's in your favor (we will get to
this later on), but if you owe it to the bank, it's the kind of fairy tale villain your
wallet does not need. So, get rid of your debt as fast as possible!

Budgeting Tips and Tricks

Now that you've got a fun snapshot of your financial standing, let's roll up our
sleeves and dive into some Budgeting Tips and Tricks. Get ready to transform your
finances with some savvy strategies that make managing money as exciting as
planning your next vacation!

Track Every Penny: Use apps, spreadsheets, or even an old-school notebook.
The first step to gaining control is understanding where your money is going.

Prioritize Necessities Over Wants: Your life isn't truly yours if you're always
worried about what others think, or buy things just to impress them. Prioritize
necessities over wants: whenever you're about to spend, ask yourself, "Is this a
necessity or just a want?" As long as you have debt, treat wants as "fun money"
and limit it to 5-10% of your income. The rest should cover your needs (like
housing, groceries, and bills), savings, and debt repayment. This way, you ensure
essentials are taken care of and you're tackling debt head-on. Adjust this to fit
your lifestyle. Oh, and by the way, eating out or ordering in falls squarely in the
"wants" category, so plan those splurges wisely!

Emergency Fund: Start with a small goal, like saving $1,000. Once you've paid
off your debts (excluding your mortgage), aim to save three to six months' worth of
expenses. This will serve as your financial safety net for unexpected expenses, such
as a broken washing machine or car repairs.

Debt Repayment: To tackle your debts with style, you have two fabulous options. First, you can use the "Snowball Method" by tackling the smallest debt first and gradually moving on to the larger ones. This gives you the joy of quick wins — like knocking out that pesky store card debt—before moving on to larger ones. Celebrate each time you eliminate a debt! This quick win boosts your motivation and keeps you moving confidently towards financial freedom.

Alternatively, you can adopt the "Avalanche Method," which focuses on eliminating the debt with the highest interest rate first. This strategy saves you more money in the long run by reducing the amount of interest you pay. Think of it as tackling the biggest fashion faux pas in your wardrobe first, ensuring you save the most while looking your best. Both methods work, so choose the one that suits your style.

Set Realistic Goals: Dream big, but plan practically. Aim for achievable savings targets and watch your small victories add up.

Automate Your Savings: Schedule regular transfers to your savings account. Out of sight, out of mind, but your future self will thank you!

Review and Adjust: Life changes, and so should your budget. Regularly review your spending and tweak your budget to stay on top of your game.

Budgeting doesn't have to be a chore. Think of it as a way to gain control over your finances and make your money work for you. By knowing where your money goes, cutting unnecessary expenses, and paying off debt, you can start building a solid financial foundation. And remember, every little bit helps. So, grab that financial selfie stick, take a good look at your money, and start budgeting like a boss. Because you deserve to live your best life—without financial stress.

Chapter 3

From Tulips to Tickers: The Glamorous Evolution of the Market

Imagine your friend found a brand-new tech company. First, the company pitches its brilliant idea to investors, giving them the chance to hop on board this exciting startup train. These investors sponsor the company's Initial Public Offering (IPO), launching the company onto the official public market. Now, any company or individual who thinks this tech company could be the next big thing can buy a share (or stock) in it. Owning a share makes the investor a partial owner of the company, kind of like having a golden ticket to Willy Wonka's Chocolate Factory – but for tech!

These investments help the company grow and develop. As the company continues to succeed, more people notice its potential and jump at the chance to buy its stocks. This growing interest drives even more demand and excitement. As demand for the stock increases, so does its price, making the investors feel like they've struck gold. This price increase not only benefits the investors but also boosts the company's value.

For the company, this growing interest is like rocket fuel, propelling it to launch more initiatives and increase its market value. So, everyone's a winner – investors feel like savvy geniuses, and the company continues to thrive and innovate.

That said, if investors see the company losing value, they might decide to sell their shares (stocks) to lock in a profit before things get worse. As more and more people sell off stocks, the demand for the company's shares drops, dragging the stock price down with it – and there goes the company's value, tumbling like a Jenga tower. This can leave investors with big losses unless the stock prices bounce back like a yo-yo.

This constant tug-of-war between supply and demand is influenced by numerous factors. Companies can't escape the inevitable market forces, such as evolving production techniques, emerging technologies, fluctuating material prices, and changing labor costs. Investors might also worry about new laws and trade policies, shifts in leadership, broader economic changes, and unfavorable publicity. And of course, the possibility that numerous investors might want to cash out their profits for personal milestones, like buying a dream home or preparing for a comfortable retirement.

So, while the stock market can be a wild ride, understanding these ups and downs can help investors hang on tight and make the best of the journey!

These various factors generate daily fluctuations in the market, making companies appear more or less successful. When a company seems to lose value, it often leads to investors jumping ship, which can actually cause the company to lose real value. It's a bit like a confidence game – human trust in the market can spark anything from economic booms to significant crises. This tricky-to-track variable is why this book focuses on finding reliable long-term investments instead of chasing quick cash.

Stocks are no longer just for the wealthy and influential. With the help of the internet and numerous accessible brokers, anyone can invest in the stock market just like a big-shot investor. There's a reason finance and investing create more millionaires than any other industry. As more people dive into the nitty-gritty of this complex system, they're crafting their own financial freedom—one smart investment at a time. Who knew learning about stocks could be the ticket to ditching the 9-to-5 grind? Let's dive in and see how you can join this exclusive club!

Now that you have a snapshot of the stock market—a dynamic place where buyers and sellers trade ownership in businesses—let's take a step back and explore how it all began. Understanding the evolution of the stock market will give you a richer appreciation for how it operates today and how it became the powerhouse of opportunity it is now. So, let's journey through time and see how the stock market has grown and transformed into the financial hub we know today.

The Dutch Are Coming!
Our story kicks off in the early 17th century with the Dutch East India Company in the Netherlands. Picture this: it's 1602, and a bunch of savvy Dutch merchants decide they need a way to raise money for their spice-trading adventures. What do they do? They invent the first-ever stock market! Investors could buy shares in the company, and in return, they'd get a slice of the profits. Voila! The Amsterdam Stock Exchange was born, and with it, the concept of trading stocks.

The Tulip Mania

In the early 17th century Netherlands, tulips became a symbol of wealth and status, sparking a frenzy of trading. Tulip prices soared to absurd heights, with some bulbs fetching more than the price of a house. This speculative bubble reached its peak in the 1630s, with people trading everything they owned for rare tulip bulbs. The market crashed in 1637, as people realized paying astronomical prices for flowers wasn't sustainable. Prices plummeted, leaving many financially ruined. Tulip Mania is a classic example that warns against the risks of speculative bubbles and the importance of evaluating an investment's real value.

London Calling

Jump ahead to the late 17th century, and we find ourselves in the bustling streets of London. The Royal Exchange is where the action's at, but it's not all tea and crumpets. Brokers and traders are making deals in coffee shops, the original hipster hangouts. Enter the South Sea Company, which promised investors untold riches from trade with South America. Spoiler alert: it was all hot air. The South Sea Bubble burst in 1720, leaving investors penniless and the market in chaos. Lesson learned: if it sounds too good to be true, it probably is.

Across the Pond

Jumping over to the United States, we land in the late 18th century. The Buttonwood Agreement of 1792 marked the birth of what would become the New York Stock Exchange (NYSE). Picture 24 stockbrokers standing under a buttonwood tree on Wall Street, agreeing to trade securities for a commission. It's humble beginnings, but hey, from tiny acorns mighty oaks grow.

The Roaring Twenties

Let's dance our way to the 1920s, the era of jazz, flappers, and economic optimism. Everyone and their dog was investing in the stock market, convinced that stock prices would keep going up forever. Cue the ominous music. In October 1929, the party came to a screeching halt with the infamous Wall Street Crash, also known as Black Tuesday. It was like the ultimate hangover, leading to the Great Depression. People realized that investing wasn't just fun and games; it required wisdom and caution.

Post-War Boom and Beyond

After World War II, the stock market experienced a post-war boom. It was the age of prosperity, suburban homes, and the baby boom. Stocks were back in vogue, and the market grew steadily. But it wasn't all smooth sailing. The market faced ups and downs, including the 1987 crash, known as Black Monday, when the Dow Jones Industrial Average plummeted by 22% in a single day. Yikes!

The Dot-Com Bubble

Now, let's fast forward to the late 1990s. The internet was the new frontier, and dot-com companies were popping up like mushrooms after the rain. Investors were throwing money at anything with a ".com" in its name. It was a frenzy! But like all good parties, this one ended with a bang. The dot-com bubble burst in 2000, wiping out trillions of dollars in market value. The lesson? Just because it's online doesn't mean it's gold.

The 2008 Financial Crisis

In 2008, we faced the financial crisis, or as some like to call it, the Great Recession. It started with the housing market collapse and spread like wildfire. Banks failed, the stock market tanked, and people were left holding the bag. It was a stark reminder that the market can be as unpredictable as a cat on catnip.

The Modern Market

Today, the stock market is a complex, global beast, with trades happening in nanoseconds thanks to technology. We've got high-frequency trading, ETFs, and cryptocurrencies—oh my! Entire schools, careers, and even dedicated television channels revolve around the stock market. It's a far cry from those Dutch merchants and their spice trades.

But through it all, the core principles remain the same: invest wisely, diversify, and don't put all your eggs in one basket. The stock market has evolved from coffeehouse deals to digital trading floors, but the goal is still to grow wealth and achieve financial freedom. So, whether you're trading in your pajamas or keeping an eye on the latest trends, remember—smart investing can turn those pennies into a fortune!

Some Basic Terms to Snack On

Stocks and Shares: When you buy a stock, you're buying a tiny piece of a company, also known as a share. Think of it as owning a slice of a giant pizza. The size of your slice depends on the number of shares you have compared to the total number of shares there are.

Shareholder: A shareholder is someone who owns shares or stock in a company, making them a partial owner of that company. Shareholders get to vote on significant company decisions and may receive dividends if the company distributes profits. Essentially, being a shareholder means having a stake in the company's success.

Public Companies: Not all businesses are in the stock market. Only public companies, which have gone through a process called an Initial Public Offering (IPO), are listed. This means they've sold a portion of their company to the public in exchange for capital to grow their business.

Yield: Yield is the income you earn from an investment, shown as a percentage. For example, if you buy a stock for $100 and it pays $5 in dividends in a year, the yield is 5%. Think of yield as the juicy fruit your investment tree produces each year. If your $100 apple tree gives you $5 worth of apples, your tree's yield is 5%.

Dividend: A dividend is a payment that a company gives to its shareholders, usually taken from its profits. It's a way for the company to share its success with the people who own its stock. Dividends are typically paid out regularly, like quarterly or annually. Think of dividends as the company giving you a slice of its profit pie—it's their way of saying, "Thanks for sticking with us; here's some pie!"

How It Works

Exchanges: Stock trading takes place on exchanges such as the New York Stock Exchange (NYSE) and NASDAQ. These are like giant supermarkets for stocks, where buying and selling happen.

Trading: Trading stocks can be done through a stockbroker or online trading platforms. When you decide to buy or sell a stock, your order goes to the exchange, where it's matched with a buyer or seller. If someone wants to sell their shares for the price you're willing to pay, the trade is made.

Prices: Stock prices fluctuate based on supply and demand. The stock price goes up when more people want to buy it than sell it. If more people want to sell than buy, the price goes down. Prices are also influenced by factors like company performance, investor sentiment, and global economic conditions.

Why It Matters

Investment and Growth: For companies, the stock market is a way to raise money to expand their business, innovate, and grow. For investors, it's an opportunity to earn a return on their money by buying stocks that increase in value over time or pay dividends (a portion of a company's earnings).

Ownership and Voting Rights: Holding stock typically grants you voting rights on company decisions during shareholder meetings. While you might not have enough shares to sway a vote, it's still a way to have a say in the company's future.

Risks and Rewards

Rewards: Investing in the stock market can lead to substantial financial gains if you pick the right stocks. Over the long term, the stock market has historically provided higher returns than many other types of investments.

Risks: However, the stock market is also risky. Prices can be volatile, and you can lose money if the companies you invest in don't perform well or if the market takes a downturn.

What Else (besides Stocks) Can Be Traded on the Stock Market?

Bonds: Bonds are essentially IOUs ("I Owe You") issued by companies or governments. When you buy a bond, you're lending money to the issuer in exchange for regular interest payments and the return of your principal at maturity. Think of bonds as lending money to your reliable but slightly boring friend, who promises to pay you back with a little interest for the favor. Unlike your friend who might spend it all on pizza, companies and governments use it for projects and expenses.

Mutual Funds: Mutual funds combine money from various investors to purchase a diverse range of stocks, bonds, or other securities, managed by professional fund managers. This allows investors to access a wide range of investments with less risk and effort than buying individual securities. Think of it as joining a financial potluck, where everyone contributes to create a diverse and well-managed investment spread.

Exchange-Traded Funds (ETFs): ETFs are similar to mutual funds but trade like stocks on an exchange. They offer diversification with the flexibility of trading throughout the day. Because ETFs are not actively managed, they usually have lower expense fees. ETFs are like those mix-and-match cereal packs. You get a variety of flavors (investments) in one package, and you can buy and sell them whenever you want.

Options: Options provide you with the ability, but not the requirement, to buy or sell a stock at a specific price within a certain period. It's like making a small down payment to keep the option of buying something later. Think of options as reserving a table at a popular restaurant. You're not sure if you'll actually show up for dinner, but it's nice to have the option just in case you crave sushi that night.

Futures: Futures contracts obligate you to buy or sell an asset at a predetermined price at a specified time in the future. It's like making a binding promise to buy something at a set price, no matter what.

Imagine you're a coffee shop owner worried about rising coffee bean prices.

You enter a futures contract to buy beans at $2 per pound six months from now. If prices skyrocket to $5 per pound, you're sipping lattes with a smug smile, having locked in the cheaper price. If prices drop to $1, well, you're still paying $2 but at least you've secured your caffeine fix without the daily grind of market worries!

Real Estate Investment Trusts (REITs): REITs allow you to invest in real estate without actually buying property. They own and manage a portfolio of real estate properties and pay dividends to investors. They're like investing in a giant real estate Monopoly game. You get a share of the rent from properties like hotels and malls without having to fix leaky roofs or deal with tenants.

Commodities: Commodities are physical goods like gold, silver, oil, and agricultural products. You can invest in them directly or through commodity ETFs and futures.

Currencies (Forex): The foreign exchange market (Forex) is where currencies are traded. Investors speculate on the relative value of currency pairs, like the euro against the dollar. Forex trading is like playing a global guessing game where you bet on which country's money will get stronger. It's like trying to predict which team will win the World Cup but with dollars and euros instead of soccer balls.

Cryptocurrencies: Cryptocurrencies are digital currencies that use cryptography for security, making them hard to counterfeit. They operate on decentralized networks based on blockchain technology, which ensures transparency and immutability of transactions. Bitcoin and Ethereum are among the most well-known examples of cryptocurrencies, and they can be used for various transactional and investment purposes. Cryptocurrencies are like the rebellious teenagers of the financial world—digital money that ditches the banks and parties on the blockchain instead!

Who Oversees the Stock Markets?

The stock exchanges themselves have a role in monitoring and regulating their own trading environments with providing a platform for buying and selling securities and ensure orderly trading, while setting rules for listing companies and monitor trading to prevent fraud and manipulation.

Navigating the stock market can still feel like walking through a jungle, and every jungle needs its rangers to keep things in check. So, who are the rangers overseeing the wild world of stock markets? Let's break it down in an easy-to-understand way.

The Securities and Exchange Commission (SEC): Think of the SEC as the big boss of the U.S. stock markets. They're the ones making sure everyone plays by the rules. The SEC's main job is to protect investors, keep the markets fair and efficient, and help businesses raise money. They oversee securities exchanges, brokers, and investment advisors. Additionally, they enforce securities laws, which means they have the authority to investigate and take legal action against those who violate the rules. So to ensure everyone plays fairly, the SEC steps in, much like the hall monitor of Wall Street, keeping a watchful eye to call out any mischief, ensuring no one runs in the halls, cheats on their homework, or sells fake hall passes.

The Financial Industry Regulatory Authority (FINRA): FINRA is a self-regulatory organization that works under the SEC's supervision. FINRA regulates brokerage firms and exchange markets. They ensure that anyone selling securities (like stocks and bonds) to the public is qualified and acts fairly. They write and enforce rules for brokers, educate investors, and resolve disputes. Think of FINRA as the stock market's referee, blowing the whistle on any fouls and making sure everyone plays fair.

The Federal Reserve (The Fed): While the Fed's primary role is monetary policy, they have significant influence over financial markets. The Fed controls the money supply and interest rates, which can have a big impact on the stock market. They manage inflation, supervise and regulate banks, and provide financial services. Picture the Fed as the wizard behind the curtain, pulling levers to control the flow of money in the economy. They might not oversee stocks directly, but their spells (or interest rate decisions) can cause market magic or mayhem.

State Securities Regulators: Each U.S. state has its own securities regulator to oversee local financial markets and protect investors. These regulators enforce state securities laws and help protect investors from fraud. They license brokerage firms and investment advisors operating within the state. Think of them as the local sheriffs of the financial Wild West, keeping the peace in their own towns (or states).

International Organizations: Outside the U.S., other countries have their own regulatory bodies, and there are international organizations to ensure cooperation across borders, such as the UK's Financial Conduct Authority (FCA), the European Securities and Markets Authority (ESMA), and India's Securities and Exchange Board (SEBI). These organizations set rules and regulations for their respective markets and work together to ensure global market stability. You can think of them as an international team of superhero regulators, each protecting their own cities but coming together to fight global financial crime.

In the end, the stock markets and Wall Street are overseen by a network of regulators and organizations working together to ensure fairness, transparency, and investor protection. From the SEC and FINRA in the U.S. to international bodies across the globe, these entities are the guardians of the financial galaxy, keeping the markets running smoothly and keeping the bad guys at bay.

PART II

Crafting Your Investment Masterplan:
Or, How to Stop Wingin' It and Start Stacking Cash

Chapter 4

Goal Digger: Setting Investment Goals That Excite You

"Most people overestimate what they can do in a year and underestimate what they can do in a decade."
- Bill Gates, the co-founder of Microsoft.

Alright, let's get real about your fabulous future! What gets your heart racing? Is it living in that dream home in the middle of calming rolling hills with a breathtaking ocean view? Jet-setting around the globe, uploading envy-worthy pics from Paris cafés and Bali beaches? Or maybe it's being able to snag that stunning designer bag without a second thought?

It's time to set investment goals that will get you excited. Think big, plan smart, and let's make those dreams come true in style!

Setting specific and motivating financial goals is like giving your money a refreshing transformation. Instead of just saying "I want to save," you're saying, "I'm saving $10,000 for a down payment on a chic new condo in two years." It's like going from "I should eat healthier" to "I'm ditching carbs for that killer dress."

When your goals are clear and exciting, it's easier to track your progress. It's like following a skincare routine: you can see those wrinkles fading (ahem, debt shrinking) each month. Plus, knowing you're working towards something fabulous, like funding your dream vacation or early retirement, keeps you going even when shopping sales are calling your name.

Having specific goals helps you make smart decisions. It's like choosing between a closet full of sale items you'll never wear and investing in a few timeless pieces. Motivating goals keep you on track and away from those impulse buys (hello, online shopping at 2 AM).

And let's talk accountability. Setting milestones is like planning your workouts with a friend—you're less likely to bail when someone (or something) is holding you accountable. Plus, the thought of reaching that goal (like finally buying that designer handbag guilt-free) keeps you disciplined.

In the end, specific and motivating goals bring financial stability and peace of mind. It's like having a perfectly organized handbag where you can find everything you need. You'll be ready for anything life tosses your way, be it an unexpected expense or an impromptu girls' trip.

So, set those goals, girl! Your financial future will thank you—and you'll look fabulous doing it.

Did you write down your dreams and how you want your future to look? Did it include dragging yourself to work with the worst flu ever just because you're out of sick days? I bet not! I'm guessing it looked more like doing whatever makes you happy and living life to the fullest.

Well, this, my friend, is called **financial freedom**! It means having ample savings, investments, and accessible funds to maintain the lifestyle you aspire for yourself and your family. It allows you to pursue your passions, whether that's starting your own business, traveling the world, or simply enjoying life without financial stress. Essentially, it's when you have sufficient financial assets to cover your living expenses indefinitely without needing to depend on regular employment income. Let's turn those dreams into reality!

Now that you know where you want to go, first things first—we have to become financially independent. That's the step before we become financially free of any BS!

Financial independence is when you have enough wealth to live comfortably without having to rely on a paycheck from a job. This means your investments, savings, and passive income streams are sufficient to cover your living expenses and lifestyle choices, giving you the freedom to work by choice, not necessity. Imagine having your investments doing the heavy lifting, while you sip mimosas and decide what fabulous thing to do next!

To reach this dreamy state of financial freedom, it's essential to understand the various ways you can generate income. Obviously, we do not want to work the 9-5 job until we're in our 90s. Life is meant to be lived and enjoyed! So let's break down different income streams and see how we can achieve our financial goals while keeping the fun alive.

First up is **active income** – this is the money you earn from performing a service, like your salary, hourly wages, commissions, and tips. It's where you trade your time and effort for cash, like that well-known 9-5 job.

Next, we have **passive income** – this is the money that rolls in with minimal effort on your part. Examples include rental income, dividends from stocks, interest from savings accounts or bonds, and royalties from intellectual property like books or music. Passive income is like that dream friend who does all the work while you sip your favorite latte.

Then there's **portfolio income** – this comes from your investments, such as capital gains from selling stocks, bonds, or real estate, as well as dividends and interest. It's your stylish friend who knows how to make money look glamorous.

To achieve financial freedom through passive income, it's essential to understand how much you'll need to cover your living expenses comfortably. Now, let's do the math and calculate how much passive income you'll need to be financially independent!

Picture this: You've got rent, utilities, health insurance, car expenses, various insurances, food, and, of course, fun money to consider. Let's say we need around $50,000 a year to cover everything (just an example number to keep it simple, taxes and inflation excluded). I get it, the number can vary depending on where you live, but we're just working with an example.

What you really want to know is: How much money do you need, to generate $50,000 in passive income through interest, dividends, returns, etc., so you can technically say goodbye to working for a living?

Now, let's start with the current return of a Certificate of Deposit (CD), which is 4% as I'm writing this. CDs are super safe investments, but here's the kicker: with an average inflation rate also around 4%, you're not really making any headway. But, don't worry, let's break down the math to see what we're working with.

Calculation 1

Desired Annual Income: $50,000

Interest Rate: 4% (or 0.04 as a decimal)

Using the simple interest formula: Annual Income = Principal × Interest Rate

Rearrange to solve for Principal:

Principal = Annual Income / Interest Rate

Plug in the values:

$$\text{Principal} = \frac{\$50,000}{0.04}$$

Principal = $1,250,000

So, you would need $1,250,000 invested at an interest rate of 4% to generate $50,000 a year in passive income, letting you live that stress-free life!

Well, that's nice to know. But let's be honest here, you wouldn't be reading this book if you had that much money just chilling under your mattress. So, off to do some more math!

Let's say we decide to invest in an ETF with an average annual dividend yield of about 10%. How much money would we need, then? Let's break it out:

Calculation 2

Desired Annual Income: $50,000

Interest Rate: 10% (or 0.10 as a decimal)

Using the same formula as we had before, with new values:

$$\text{Principal} = \frac{\$50,000}{0.10}$$

Principal = $500,000

Alright, that looks a little better. You'd need $500,000 invested at an interest rate of 10% to generate $50,000 a year in passive income.

But, let's be real. $500,000 still seems like a pretty tall order. So, let's put on our math hats and see what we can do with a 15% return. This kind of return is possible with some high-flying stocks, right?

Calculation 3

Desired Annual Income: $50,000

Interest Rate: 15% (or 0.15 as a decimal)

Using the same formula as we had before, with new values:

$$\text{Principal} = \frac{\$50,000}{0.15}$$

Principal = $333,333.34

Now that's looking a lot more doable! Not perfect, but we can work with this. So, you'd need $333,333.34 invested at an interest rate of 15% to generate $50,000 a year in passive income. With some smart stock picks, that $333,333.34 can work its magic and bring you a step closer to living the dream without the dreaded day job.

But how do we get there, you ask? Well, remember our magical vacation funded by the ever-so-generous credit card? The one where compound interest was our evil nemesis? Let's flip the script and let compound interest be our fairy godmother this time. Abra-cadabra, let's make that money work for us!

Imagine you have a magic piggy bank that not only keeps your money safe but also has a party every month. Each month, it invites all the previous interest it earned to join the fun and make even more money babies. So, if you put $100 in this magic piggy bank with a 15% interest rate, after the first month, it earns $15 and now has $115. Next month, it earns 15% on $115, so $17.25 joins the party to make it $132,25. The cycle keeps going, and before you know it, your piggy bank is throwing the wildest, most profitable parties in town!

Let's break it down to get to the magical $333,333. Say we start with an initial $1,000, adding a fabulous $500 every month. That's $7,000 in the first year. Now, sprinkle that with a 15% interest rate, and you've got $8,050 at the end of year one. Keep this chic routine up, and in just over 15 years and 10 months, you'll hit $333,333.34.

To put it in perspective, that's way faster than a bank dragging you through decades of paying off a $333,333.34 loan for your home—with a much higher monthly payment, while also tacking on another $333,333.34 in interest costs. Yikes!

If you decide to contribute more or snag an even better return, you'll hit your wealth goals faster than you can say "shopping spree."

With your roadmap to financial independence in hand, you now get the concept and can calculate your own magic number for financial independence and financial freedom. Now, $500 might be a little much at the moment. This is just an example—start small and add as much as you can, just like you did when paying back that debt. Little savings every month are better than none at all. So, go ahead and start dreaming about your fabulous future! Picture yourself lounging at your serene lake house, far away from the daily grind, sipping tea and basking in your well-earned success. Cheers to making those dreams a reality!

Chapter 5

Shopping the Stock Market: Picking the Right Investments

The stock market is like a fashion show—always changing and full of surprises. Depending on the year, you might find yourself more in vogue with stocks, gold, bonds, or even that dazzling new accessory, crypto. But darling, to show off your stuff on this financial runway, you need to know the trends and the designers behind them. This fabulous book will be your guide to the stock market, teaching you how to invest and analyze stocks with the finesse of a seasoned fashionista. You'll learn how to spot high-quality companies with strong management, consistent earnings, and a competitive edge—basically, the Chanel of stocks that you can flaunt forever. So, grab your financial stilettos, and let's turn those investments into the next big thing!

Charts & Charms: Stock Charts for the Savvy Woman

Before diving into stock analysis, it's essential to understand what we're looking at and where to find the necessary information. Let's get comfortable with stock charts, which are crucial tools in analyzing stock performance.

What is a Stock Chart?

A stock chart is a graphical representation of a stock's price movements over time. It shows how the price has changed and helps identify trends and patterns. The key components are the Price Axis, Time Axis, Candlesticks/Bars, and Volume. I will explain this to you in a later chapter. For now, we will just be looking at the stock movements.

Stock charts can be easily found online on financial websites like Yahoo Finance, Google Finance, Tradingview, and brokerage platforms. These sites provide interactive charts that allow you to customize the time frame and view detailed information. Just like shopping for the best deal online, you can compare and analyze stocks efficiently.

As an example, I added three companies from the beauty sector. For a well-diversified portfolio and to spread your risks, you'll want to include stocks from about three to five different sectors. It's like having a wardrobe with everything from casual to formal wear—you need variety to be ready for any occasion!

What's a Sector?

Think of a sector as a way to group companies into different neighborhoods based on what they do. It helps investors figure out which part of the economy a company belongs to. Here's a fun breakdown of the various sectors, each buzzing with companies doing similar things:

Energy: Think of big names like Exxon Mobil Corporation (XOM), Chevron Corporation (CVX), this sector is all about the production and distribution of energy, covering everything from oil and gas to renewable energy sources. They keep the world powered up!

Materials: DuPont de Nemours Inc. (DD) and Dow Inc. (DOW) are well-known examples here. These companies produce raw materials like chemicals, metals, and paper, which are essential for manufacturing and construction. They're the suppliers of the building blocks for many industries.

Industrials: Company giants like Caterpillar Inc. (CAT) and General Electric Co (GE) are in this sector. It includes companies that produce goods and provide services used in construction, manufacturing, and industrial applications. They make the heavy-duty stuff that keeps industries running.

Aerospace and Defense: This sector includes companies involved in manufacturing aircraft, like Boeing Co. (BA), defense systems, such as Lockheed Martin Corp. (LMT), and other aerospace products. They're the high-flyers and protectors.

Consumer Discretionary: Amazon.com Inc. (AMZN) is one of the rock stars of this sector. These companies produce non-essential goods and services — think automobiles, entertainment, and retail. They cater to our wants and whims.

Consumer Staples: This sector covers companies that produce essential goods and services like food, beverages, and household products. These are the everyday items you can't live without. Procter & Gamble Co. (PG) and Coca-Cola Co. (KO) are literally the staples in this sector. Other key players include Costco Wholesale

Corporation (COST) and Walmart Inc. (WMT).

Healthcare: Johnson & Johnson (JNJ), Eli Lilly and Company (LLY) and Pfizer (PFE) are leading players in the pharmaceutical industry, and therefore in the Healthcare sector. This sector involves companies that provide healthcare services, pharmaceuticals, biotechnology, and medical equipment.

Financials: This sector includes companies providing financial services such as banking, investment firms, and insurance. They're the money movers and shakers, with notable companies like JPMorgan Chase (JPM) and Bank of America Corporation (BAC).

Information Technology: Microsoft Corp. (MSFT), Apple Inc. (AAPL), and NVIDIA Corp. (NVDA) lead the charge here. This sector encompasses companies that develop or distribute tech products and services, including software, hardware, and IT services. They're the tech wizards.

Telecommunication Services: The companies in this field provide communication services, including telephone, internet, and wireless communication. They keep us all connected. AT&T Inc. (T) and Verizon Communications Inc. (VZ) are leaders in the telecommunication services space.

Utilities: This sector covers companies that provide essential services like electricity, water, and natural gas. They're the utility superheroes keeping the lights on. Vistra Corp (VST) and Constellation Energy Corporation (CEG) are prime examples, consistently delivering reliable power to millions. Other notable names in this sector include Duke Energy (DUK) and Southern Company (SO), ensuring we stay powered up and comfortable, no matter the season.

Real Estate: This sector involves companies that manage, develop, and invest in residential, commercial, and industrial properties. They're the real estate moguls. American Tower Corp. (AMT) and Simon Property Group Inc. (SPG) are key players, as well as Prologis Inc. (PLD) and Strawberry Fields REIT (STRW).

Communication Services: You might be familiar with these names: Facebook, now known as Meta Platforms Inc. (META), Netflix Inc. (NFLX), and Google, also known as Alphabet Inc. (GOOGL). These companies provide media, entertainment, and information services, dominating the digital and media landscapes. From social networking and streaming entertainment to search engines and online advertising, they shape the way we interact with technology and consume content. Their innovative platforms and services have become essential parts of our daily lives, driving the future of digital communication and entertainment.

Understanding these sectors helps you diversify your portfolio, reduce risk, and boost potential returns. It's like having a balanced diet, but for your investments! Whether you're excited about tech or crazy about textiles, there's a sector out there just waiting for you to explore and invest in!

Having learned about market sectors, you might have spotted letters in parentheses behind their names. These are called stock symbols. Stock symbols are unique series of letters assigned to publicly traded companies. Think of them as the company's nickname in the stock market. The Walt Disney Co. goes by DIS, Tesla is TSLA, and Microsoft shows up as MSFT. We'll need these handy nicknames to check out charts, buy, or sell shares. It's like calling your bestie by their cool nickname—quicker, snappier, and perfect for navigating the stock market in style!

To get the scoop on our stock movements, we'll dive into the 5-year stock chart. When you hop onto a financial website, you can usually choose from different time frames: 1 day, 5 days, 1 month, 3 months, 6 months, Tesla, 1 year, 2 years, 5 years, or even the all-time chart. Some sites even let you pick specific dates for a custom look. For our exercise, we're all about the 5-Year Yield: this shows the percentage change in the stock's value over five years, including dividends, giving us a big-picture view of performance. For example, if a stock was $50 five years ago and is now $100, the 5-year yield is 100%.

Here's the breakdown:
- Absolute Dollar Change (+$119.43): This shows the actual increase in the stock price over five years.
- Percentage Growth (+2,908.99%): This indicates how much the stock price has skyrocketed over five years. For example, if a stock was $4.10 five years ago and is now $123.53, it's grown by a whopping 2,908.99%.

Now that we've set up our charts to the 5-year overview, let's dive into interpreting those stock movements. The horizontal line on the chart is like a timeline of your stock's life, while the vertical line shows its value in dollars. For our practice, we'll use the line chart, or mountain chart. We'll save the candlestick charts for a later chapter—trust me, they're worth the wait! So, let's get charting and see what stories these lines have to tell!

Upward Movement

When a stock chart shows an upward trend, it means the stock price is rising. This usually results from positive news, strong earnings reports, favorable economic conditions, or increased investor confidence. An upward movement suggests good performance and growth prospects, reflecting investor optimism about the company's future. This is exactly what we're looking for to make money. Just like finding the perfect pair of shoes on sale, it's a reason to celebrate!

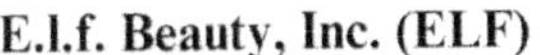

E.l.f. Beauty, Inc. (ELF)

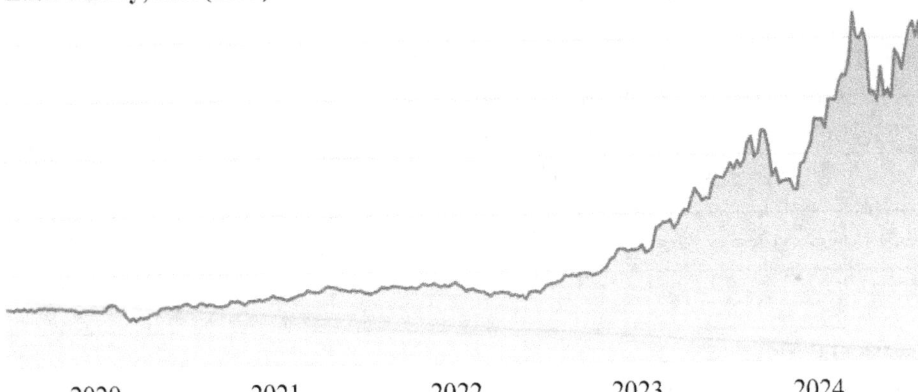

Over the past five years, e.l.f. Beauty (ELF) has shown impressive upward movement, with its stock price reflecting significant growth. The company's revenue jumped from $578.84 million in 2022 to $1.02 billion in 2023, marking a 76.89% increase, and earnings soared by 107.48% to $127.66 million. This strong financial performance has boosted investor confidence and market performance, akin to finding your favorite lipstick back in stock after a major sale—a sign of good things ahead.

Downward Movement

A downward trend on a stock chart indicates the stock price is falling. This can result from negative news, poor earnings reports, unfavorable economic conditions, or decreased investor confidence. It often implies concerns about the company's performance or future prospects, signaling investor pessimism or a reaction to bad news. It's like realizing your favorite fashion label uses child labor to produce their clothes—definitely not the news you wanted to hear!

Revlon Inc. (REVRQ)

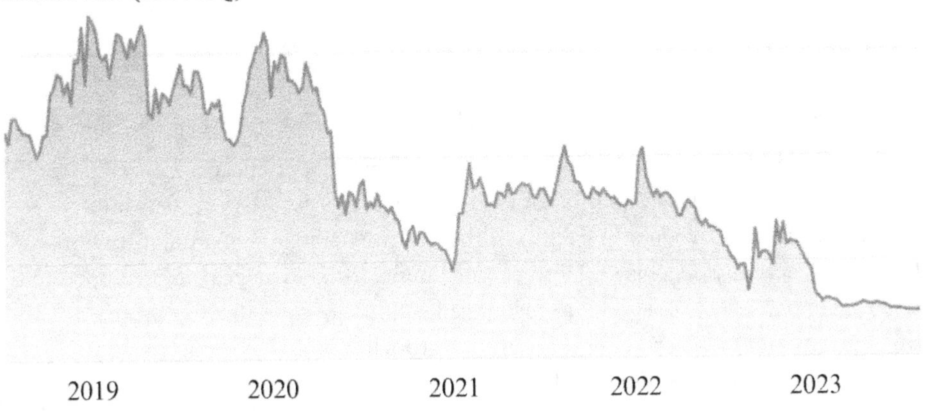

The past five years, Revlon Inc. (REVRQ) has had quite the rollercoaster ride with its stock performance. The company battled declining revenues and increasing losses, thanks to supply chain hiccups and higher operational costs. In 2022, their revenue slipped to $1.98 billion, down 4.73% from the previous year, and losses hit $673.9 million. Things got so rough that they filed for Chapter 11 bankruptcy, but by 2023, they emerged with less debt and new owners. Despite all this drama, Revlon is still in the game, trying to get back on track. Navigating Revlon's stock over these years has been like mastering winged eyeliner—tricky, but oh-so-satisfying when you get it just right!

Horizontal Movement

When a stock chart shows horizontal movement, it means the stock price is stable with little change. This can happen because the market is undecided, supply and demand are balanced, or there's just no big news affecting the stock. While this suggests a stable condition, it's not a stock we want to invest in. The lack of growth, coupled with the inflation rate, means you might actually lose money on the deal. It's like being stuck in traffic with no movement in sight—not the best use of your time or money!

Ulta Beauty, Inc. (ULTA)

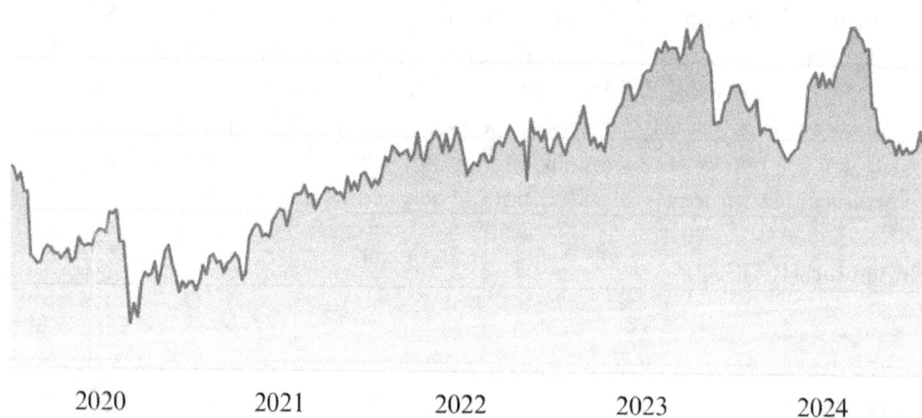

Over the past five years, ULTA Beauty's stock has experienced a largely horizontal movement, with a modest overall increase of just 4.18%. This limited growth means that, when adjusted for inflation, the real value of an investment in ULTA has actually decreased. Despite some highs from strong earnings reports and strategic expansions, the stock has also faced significant lows due to market fluctuations and increased competition. Investors holding ULTA have essentially seen a roller coaster ride that, in the end, left them not much better off than where they started. Nonetheless, ULTA's strong brand presence and customer loyalty suggest potential for future growth.

Up, down, and horizontal movement—easy peasy, right? But wait, there's more! Stock charts are like the Swiss Army knives of finance; they can also help you uncover the growth phases of a company. Curious about where a company is in its lifespan? Let's hit that "all-time" time frame and dive in. Reading the growth phases of a company on a stock chart is like following the plot of a thrilling story. Here's how you can interpret the different chapters of this financial saga:

Glam Guide to Growth: Business Phases Every Woman Should Know

Start-Up Phase (Baby and Small Child Phase): Imagine a start-up as a newborn — adorable and full of potential, but needing a lot of care and attention. This phase is all about high risk and high reward. The company is just getting started, focusing on creating its product, entering the market, and attracting those first precious customers. It's like a whirlwind of activity, with constant adjustments and new challenges every day.

During this time, research and development are the main focus, requiring both significant effort and funding. Think of it as the company learning to crawl, walk, and eventually run. While the idea of getting in early on the next Microsoft or Apple sounds exciting, it's crucial to remember that most start-ups don't make it past this stage. Investing in a start-up without being deeply involved is a bit like buying a lottery ticket — thrilling, but incredibly risky.

For those of us aiming for steady financial returns, start-up investments might not be the best fit due to these high risks. It's a wild ride, and unless you're ready to be hands-on, it's better to look for more stable opportunities.

Growth Phase (The Teenager Stage): Welcome to the teenage years of a company's life — full of energy, rapid growth, and a few awkward growing pains. In the growth phase, companies see their revenue, market share, and geographic reach expand quickly. It's like watching a teenager sprout up overnight, suddenly needing bigger clothes and more space.

These companies are busy reinvesting their profits to keep the growth momentum going. They hire more staff, boost production, and dive into new markets. But just like teenagers, they encounter some bumps along the way — operational hiccups, the need for more sophisticated management, and occasional cash flow dramas.

To thrive, companies in this phase must keep innovating and adapting to market demands. It's a time for refining their business models and developing more mature processes. Implementing better control systems and establishing a structured organizational framework are crucial to handle the increased complexity.

Cultural shifts are inevitable, and leadership must manage these transitions to keep the workforce motivated. During this phase, the business is defining its long-term identity and market position, much like a teenager figuring out who they are. Proving the sustainability and profitability of the business model on a larger scale is essential, as is effective resource management of financial, human, and technological assets.

Investing in companies during the growth phase can be very appealing. They've moved beyond the risky start-up stage and are poised for significant returns through their expanding market presence and profitability. It's an exciting time to get on board and watch the company come into its own.

Maturity Phase (The Adult Stage): In the maturity phase, also known as the adult stage of a company's lifecycle. Imagine a company that's done with the wild roller-coaster rides of its youth and is now cruising along smoothly, like a seasoned professional who's got it all together. Growth rates might slow down, but this company is the reliable, successful adult in the room, with a solid market presence and plenty of stability.

At this stage, the company often holds a significant share of the market and is recognized as a leader in its industry. Think of it as the go-to expert everyone trusts. With strong brand recognition and customer loyalty, it generates consistent revenue and profits through well-established revenue streams. Operations are streamlined and efficient, with an ongoing focus on cost control and process optimization. While the rapid growth spurts of youth are behind it, the company still invests in innovation to stay competitive and meet changing market demands.

Growth rates may slow down since the company has already captured a large portion of the market, facing increased competition and the need to differentiate itself. Now, the focus shifts to long-term strategic planning — think diversification, mergers, and acquisitions. Sustainable practices and creating long-term value for shareholders become key priorities.

In this phase, companies often return profits to shareholders through dividends or share buybacks. While these companies offer stable revenues and lower risk, they might not be as thrilling for us high-growth seekers, since the explosive growth stage is behind them, resulting in lower yields for our investment.

In summary, the maturity phase represents a time when a company is fully developed, established, and operates with a high degree of stability and efficiency. While the growth opportunities may be less pronounced than in earlier stages, the focus shifts to maintaining market position, optimizing operations, and creating long-term value. This phase offers potential for steady returns but limited growth, making it ideal for those seeking stability and reliability.

Decline Phase (The Retirement Stage): The decline phase, often referred to as the "retirement" stage of a company. Imagine this phase as the twilight years, where the company faces decreasing revenues, market share, and profitability. It's like the corporate equivalent of realizing you can't party like you used to. Market saturation, increased competition, or shifts in consumer preferences are the culprits behind this slowdown, leading to significant challenges and heightened risks.

In this stage, market saturation often results in dwindling sales as the demand for the company's products or services fades away. Think of it as the once-popular disco dance now struggling to find a crowd. Technological advancements or changes in consumer tastes can make the company's offerings feel like yesterday's news. Shrinking profit margins are common, driven by lower sales volumes and potentially higher costs. If the company can't keep expenses in check or discover new revenue streams, it may start experiencing losses faster than a retiree spending their savings on cruise vacations.

To cope with these financial pressures, companies might need to cut costs through layoffs, facility closures, or reduced operations. In some cases, they might have to sell off assets to manage cash flow and debts — like a retiree downsizing from a mansion to a cozy cottage. Management may also consider exit strategies such as selling the company, merging with another firm, or declaring bankruptcy. Products or services that are no longer profitable might be discontinued, much like retiring outdated hobbies.

Despite these challenges, some companies attempt a comeback by innovating or diversifying into new markets or products. Rebranding or repositioning efforts may also be undertaken to regain market interest, akin to a retiree taking up a new, trendy hobby. However, if recovery proves unfeasible, the company may eventually close down operations, managing its legacy and ensuring any remaining obligations to stakeholders are met — kind of like tidying up affairs and saying goodbye gracefully.

In summary, the decline stage presents numerous challenges as the company struggles to maintain its market position and financial health. Strategic decisions made during this stage can determine whether the company will successfully navigate its decline, potentially finding new paths to growth, or ultimately exiting the market with dignity.

Let's have a look at some real life examples:

Analyzing Amazon.com's (AMZN) Start-Up Phase: In this chart, you can observe Amazon.com's start-up phase, characterized by rapid and volatile price movements, low trading volumes, and sharp spikes or drops.

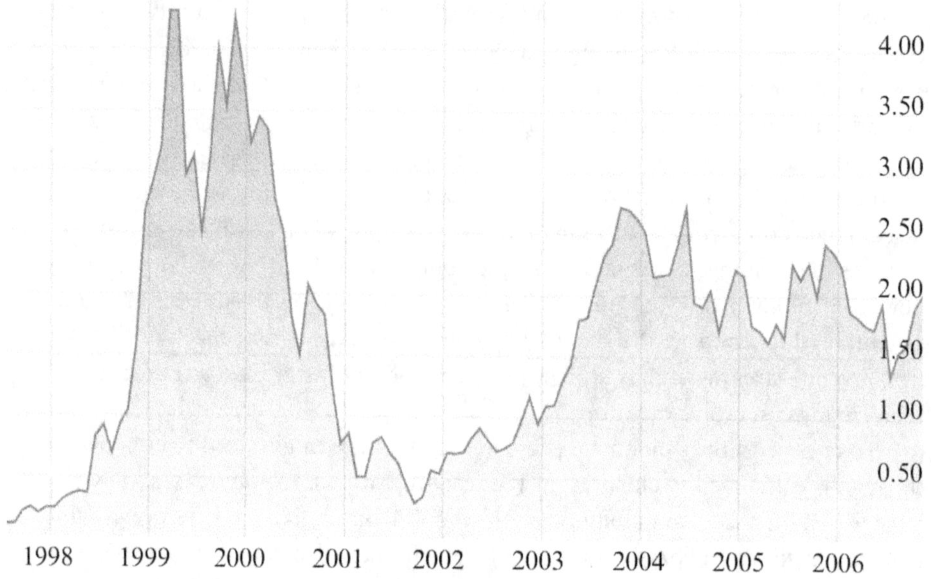

Here are the key indicators that define this phase:

- **Low and Unsteady Prices:** During the start-up phase, stock prices are generally low and fluctuate significantly. This is due to the company's early stage of development and the uncertainty surrounding its future prospects.
- **High Volatility:** Frequent, sharp price movements occur due to market speculation and low liquidity. Investors are often reacting to new information and trying to gauge the potential success of the company.
- **Volume Spikes:** You'll notice occasional spikes in trading volume, usually coinciding with major announcements or product launches. These spikes indicate heightened investor interest and activity as the market reacts to new developments.

It's important to remember that Amazon was not profitable for the first few years of its existence. Despite its promising business model, the company initially focused on growth and market share, leading to significant investments and expenses that delayed profitability.

In summary, Amazon.com's start-up phase was like the rollercoaster of emotions during a dramatic season of your favorite TV show. Volatility was like the unpredictable fashion trends; one minute it's in, the next it's out. Just like how gossip spreads in a group chat, investor enthusiasm and market rumors could send the stock soaring or plummeting in the blink of an eye.

Analyzing Amazon.com's (AMZN) Growth Phase: In Amazon.com's growth phase, the company experienced a consistent upward trend in stock prices, increasing trading volumes, and an expanding market presence. This phase is characterized by the following indicators:

- **Upward Trend:** During the growth phase, Amazon's stock prices showed a steady increase over time. This reflects the company's growing revenues and expanding market share as it solidified its position in the e-commerce sector and diversified its offerings.
- **Higher Trading Volumes:** As Amazon continued to grow, there was increased interest from investors, leading to higher trading volumes. This indicates that more investors were buying into the company's growth potential and future prospects.
- **Short-Term Corrections:** Despite the overall upward trend, there were periodic pullbacks or corrections in Amazon's stock prices. These short-term dips were often followed by continued upward momentum, showing the market's confidence in Amazon's long-term growth trajectory.

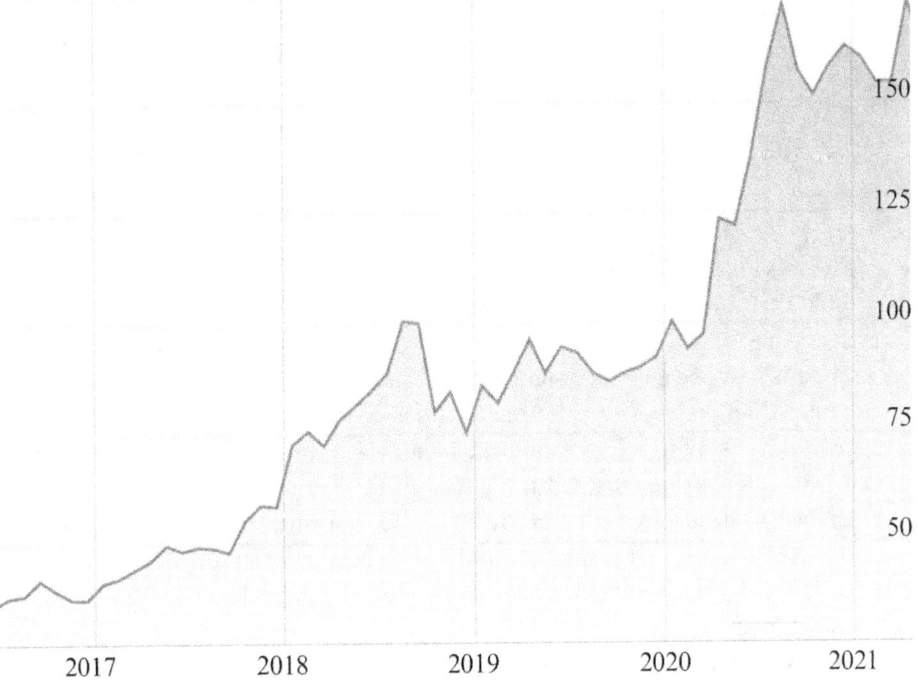

During this phase, Amazon's incredible growth was fueled by strategic reinvestments in logistics and technology, allowing it to expand operations, enter new markets, and continuously innovate. These moves not only boosted revenues but also enhanced its market presence and competitive edge.

In a nutshell, Amazon.com's growth phase was like watching your girl gang level up. Picture the gang getting more invites to the hottest parties (steady increase in stock prices), picking up fans left and right (higher trading volumes), and occasionally dealing with the drama (periodic corrections).

These moves showed that your crew was totally smashing their goals, building a squad of loyal followers (growing investor confidence), and earning their right to sit at the cool kids' table (strong market position). This phase was basically Amazon going from the new girl in town to the reigning queen of the scene!

Analyzing Mercedes-Benz Group AG (MBG) in the Maturity Phase: Let's take a closer look at Mercedes-Benz during its maturity phase, where stability and reliability are the names of the game.

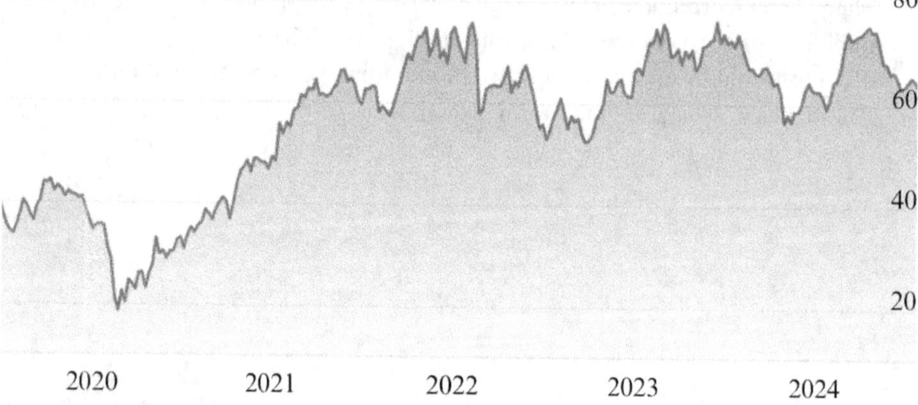

- **Stable Performance:** Think of Mercedes-Benz's stock prices as a smooth, scenic drive—they've leveled out and now move within a steady range, showing the company's strong and consistent market presence.
- **Investor Confidence:** Mercedes-Benz attracts a loyal group of investors, much like fans flocking to see their favorite band. High trading volumes reflect this ongoing interest and trust in the company's solid returns.
- **Regular Dividends:** Investing in Mercedes-Benz means getting regular dividends, like receiving quarterly bonuses. These payouts are seen in slight dips in stock prices on ex-dividend dates, showing that Mercedes-Benz values its shareholders.
- **Lower Volatility:** Compared to its earlier, more volatile years, Mercedes-Benz's

stock now shows less drama and more stability, mirroring its dependable financial performance and predictable earnings.

- **Operational Efficiency:** Mercedes-Benz has fine-tuned its operations for high efficiency and cost control. The company's strong brand and loyal customer base keep it running smoothly, much like its luxury vehicles.
- **Continued Innovation:** Even in its maturity, Mercedes-Benz keeps innovating and adapting to market changes. The focus now is on maintaining efficiency, planning for the long term, and keeping up with the latest trends.

Mercedes-Benz's maturity phase is like your dependable best friend — steady, reliable, and always there for you. Stable stock prices? Check. Regular dividends? Check. High trading volumes and lower volatility? Double check. These indicators show that Mercedes-Benz is the epitome of consistency. Investors love the company's steady performance, making it the go-to choice for reliable returns.

Analyzing Sears Holdings Corp (SHLDQ) in the Decline Phase: In this chart, you can observe Sears during its decline phase, often referred to as the retirement stage. This phase is marked by a consistent downward trend in stock prices, decreasing trading volumes, and increasing volatility.

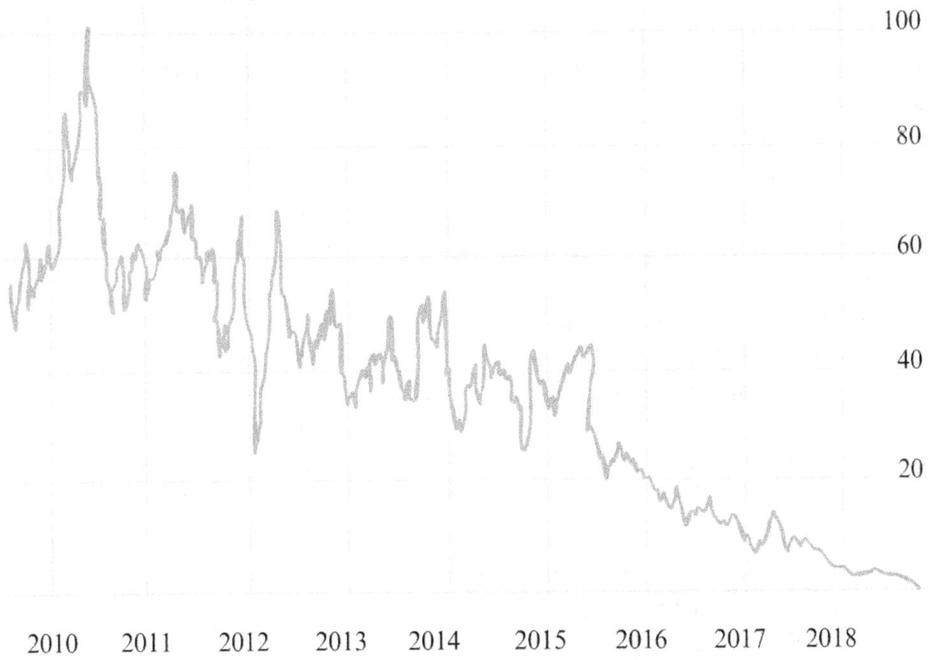

Key Characteristics and Stock Chart Indicators:
- **Downward Trend:** Sears' stock prices steadily decreased over time, reflecting declining revenues and market share.
- **Decreasing Trading Volumes:** Reduced investor interest led to lower trading volumes, signaling waning confidence in the company.
- **Increased Volatility:** Larger price swings were due to market uncertainty and negative news, making the stock unpredictable.
- **Support and Resistance Levels:** Frequent testing and breaking of support levels indicated persistent financial struggles and further declines.

Sears' decline phase showcased a steady drop in stock prices, reduced trading volumes, and heightened volatility. These indicators pointed to ongoing financial difficulties, diminishing market presence, and a lack of investor confidence. The company's inability to compete with online retailers and mounting debt worsened its decline, leading to frequent breakdowns of support levels and further reinforcing negative sentiment.

In summary, Sears' decline phase was like watching a once-iconic pop star struggle to stay relevant. The stock prices kept falling, like a hit single dropping off the charts. Trading volumes were lower than the crowd at a washed-up band's reunion tour, showing that investors had moved on to fresher acts. The increased volatility was as unpredictable as a diva's stunts on social media—always keeping everyone on edge. Frequent breakdowns of support levels were like constant bad press, each one a blow to the company's already fragile reputation and financial stability.

As you get the hang of chart movements and spotting the different phases in a company's lifetime, let's jump straight into the fun part. Can you think of some companies that might be on the stock market?

Grab your favorite notebook, because we're about to make the ultimate VIP list of as many companies you know and love. Think about your favorite coffee company, car company, clothing stores, electronics brands like phones, computers, fridges, and more. I bet you won't have any trouble coming up with names. After your initial brainstorming session, channel your inner Marie Kondo and only keep the growth-phase companies that spark joy by having a minimum growth of 100% within the last 5 years. Write down their names, stock symbols, the sector they belong to, and their 5-year performance. Then, sort them by the top performers within each sector.

After this, we'll dive deeper into our top 10-20 companies and uncover some investment gems! Think of it as decluttering your closet and keeping only the outfits that make you feel absolutely fabulous.

Bravo! You've just weeded out the not-so-glamorous stocks. Now, I'm not saying the ones we tossed won't ever have their moment on the runway, but right now, we're all about those high performers that are ready to make our wallets bling. Next, we'll get to know the fabulous companies that made the cut because, darling, you can't just rely on a pretty stock chart — there's more to these investments than meets the eye. Let's dive in and discover what makes these companies truly sparkle!

Once we've curated our elite list of 10-20 top performers, it's time to delve deeper and uncover their competitive advantages. We're all about quality over quantity here - like buying a fabulous pair of shoes that never go out of style. How valuable are these shining stars, and how secure is their ability to generate wealth?

Why You Want the Glamorous Goal of a Competitive Advantage When Picking Stocks!

A competitive advantage is like a secret weapon that allows a company to excel in its industry. This is also known as a "moat", much like a moat protects a castle. A moat safeguards a castle by surrounding it with a wide, deep ditch filled with water, making it difficult for attackers to approach and breach the walls. Likewise, in the context of stocks, a moat represents a company's competitive advantage that prevents rivals from invading on its market share. Just as a moat secures a castle, a strong competitive advantage protects a company's profitability and market position from being eroded by competitors. This concept was popularized by Warren Buffett, who uses it to describe a business's ability to maintain long-term financial success and market share.

When you invest in companies with a strong competitive advantage, you're more likely to see consistent returns and growth over time. It's like picking a winning team — you want the one with the best players, strategy, and track record. So, when choosing stocks, look for those that have something special that sets them apart and keeps them ahead of the competition.

Here are the five key criteria to spot your next stock superstar with a competitive advantage:

1. The Engine of Excellence: Patents, Processes, and Market Mastery
Does your chosen company have a secret weapon — like a recipe as iconic as Coca-Cola's or Kentucky Fried Chicken's original recipe? Does it possess unique

trademarks, cutting-edge technologies, or any other gold mines that set it apart from its competitors?

Intellectual Property: Companies that focus on protecting their trademarks and patents often have a significant competitive edge. These protected innovations and brand recognition can set them apart from others. One of the most famous examples of intellectual property is by the Coca-Cola Company (KO). The secret recipe for Coca-Cola has been a closely guarded trade secret since the company's inception. The exact formula for the Coca-Cola beverage is known by only a few people within the company, making it one of the best-kept secrets in the business world. This recipe gives Coca-Cola a unique taste that is difficult to replicate, ensuring its distinctive place in the market.

Legal Strength: Strong trademarks and patents can prevent competitors from infringing on the company's market share, safeguarding their position in the industry. Microsoft Corporation (MSFT), for example, has patents in software, cloud computing, artificial intelligence, and augmented reality. Technologies behind products like Windows, Azure, and HoloLens are safeguarded by their extensive patent portfolio.

Advanced Technology: Does the company have advanced technology that improves efficiency, product quality, or market relevance? For example, Amazon.com, Inc. (AMZN) is a leader in logistics and supply chain management, revolutionizing the retail industry with its advanced technology. Their same-day shipping service uses modern warehouse technology, robots, and smart computer programs to deliver packages quickly. This makes the process more efficient and keeps customers happy. Their technological advantage helps Amazon lead the e-commerce market.

By considering these elements, you can better understand how a company's unique strengths and intellectual properties contribute to its competitive edge, making it a true market diva, dazzling and dominating its opponents.

2. Fortune Formula: Understanding Income Streams for Success

How does the company you picked make money? Does the company offer subscriptions? If you've ever had a phone, you know the drill. Phone service costs money, whether you're yapping up a storm or going radio silent. You're always paying, and that's how companies rake in the cash. They make money from subscription fees, ensuring a steady stream of income, whether you're chatting away or just using data for your latest binge-watch session. It's a consistent cash flow, like a well-oiled machine!

Other examples include your TV streaming services, that rarely-touched gym membership, or life-saving medication from big pharma. Let's be honest, pharmaceutical companies don't make money when you're in tip-top shape; they profit when you need to take something every single day just to keep ticking.

Credit card processors are a prime example of businesses with income streams tied to nearly every purchase— except when you go old school and pay with cash. They earn their keep through transaction fees, annual card fees, and equipment leasing.

Now, let's explore how many income streams your company has. It's essential to identify and understand these different revenue sources, such as product sales, services, subscriptions, advertising, licensing, royalties, transaction fees, rent and leasing, interest and dividends, and franchise fees.

Take the Walt Disney Company (DIS) as our glittering example. Disney's got a revenue wardrobe as diverse as a fashionista's closet. They charm us with ticket sales, merchandise, and hospitality services at their dreamy theme parks. Then, they rake in the dough from advertising and subscription fees for channels like ESPN and ABC, movie ticket sales, DVDs, and streaming service Disney+.

Disney doesn't stop there — they also cash in on consumer products featuring their beloved characters, licensing their magical intellectual property, and publishing books and magazines. Disney masterfully diversifies its revenue streams across entertainment, media, consumer products, and hospitality, making sure their purse strings are always jingling.

How many income streams does your company have? Exploring and expanding these can enhance your company's financial stability and growth potential, giving it that extra sprinkle of Disney magic.

When analyzing a company, consider how they generate revenue. Is it through product sales, subscriptions, licensing deals, or perhaps all of the above? If they have multiple, reliable sources of income, you've found a potentially profitable investment. Just like Disney thrives on movies, theme parks, merchandise, and more, a company with diverse income streams is well-equipped for success.

3. The Brand Power Play: How Big Names Boost Your Bottom Line

While we're on a roll dropping big names, let's dive deeper. Do you have a favorite brand, or can you think of some iconic brand names? Is there one brand you swear by over another, and why?

Yes, you guessed it! One major way to secure a competitive advantage is by having a brand name that's recognized worldwide and carries a sterling reputation. A strong brand stands out for several reasons:

- **Quality and Reliability:** A good brand consistently delivers top-notch products or services, creating a loyal customer base. Think about brands like Apple or Nike—they've built reputations for quality and innovation.

- **Emotional Connection:** Successful brands connect with customers on an emotional level. They understand their audience's desires and needs, fostering a deep sense of loyalty. Consider how Disney's brand evokes feelings of happiness and nostalgia.
- **System Loyalty:** Brand loyalty plays a significant role in buying decisions, as consumers often stick with familiar systems like Apple or Android due to their seamless integration and consistent user experience. Switching systems can be daunting because it involves adapting to a new interface, transferring data, and potentially losing access to favorite apps or services. For instance, an iPhone user might hesitate to switch to Android due to the hassle of moving away from Apple's ecosystem, which includes iCloud, iMessage, and AirDrop. Similarly, an Android user might stay loyal to their preferred brand for its customization options and variety of device choices.
- **Consistency:** Strong brands maintain a consistent image and message across all platforms. This consistency creates trust and makes the brand easy to recognize.
- **Customer Service:** Exceptional customer service can enhance a brand's reputation. Think of how brands like Nordstrom are known for going above and beyond to satisfy their customers.
- **Innovation:** Leading brands often stay ahead of the curve by continuously innovating. They aren't afraid to take risks and set trends.

Having a globally recognized brand that people trust is like having the perfect little black dress – it never goes out of style and always makes you look good. This trust lets brands hike up their prices, leading to higher profit margins and extra cash to reinvest in staying fabulous and ahead of the competition.

So, when considering your company's competitive edge, ask yourself: Does it have that brand power? Because just like a signature handbag, a well-known, reputable brand can be a total game-changer in the business world.

4. Steering to Success: The Leadership Advantage

Let's dive into one of the most crucial aspects of any company: its leadership and management. How is the leadership team steering the ship? Does the company have a rockstar leader or visionary who commands more fans than the company has shares, much like Steve Jobs did for Apple?

Here are some key considerations:

- **Visionary Leadership:** A charismatic and forward-thinking leader can inspire confidence and attract a loyal following, both among customers and investors. These rockstar leaders often have a clear vision for the future and can drive the company towards innovation and growth.

- **Crisis Management:** How does leadership react during tough times, such as bear markets? Do they make strategic moves to protect the company, or do they continue to pay themselves excessive salaries while the company struggles? Exceptional leaders are those who demonstrate strong crisis management skills, making tough decisions for the long-term health of the company.
- **Leadership Stability:** Frequent changes in leadership, especially every 1-2 years, can be a major red flag. It often indicates internal turmoil, lack of direction, and instability, which can erode investor confidence and disrupt the company's progress. Stability in leadership often suggests a cohesive strategy and a united vision.
- **Future Vision:** What are their plans for the future of the company? Do they have a clear and compelling vision, or are they just winging it? Companies with leaders who have well-defined, ambitious, yet achievable plans are more likely to thrive in the long run.
- **Ethical Leadership:** Ethical practices and integrity are also crucial. Leaders who prioritize ethical behavior can foster a trustworthy and sustainable corporate culture, reducing the likelihood of scandals that could harm the company's reputation and financial stability.

In summary, the quality of a company's leadership is a cornerstone of its potential success. A strong, visionary leader with ethical practices, stability, and a clear future vision can make all the difference. When evaluating a company, pay close attention to who's at the helm— because let's be real, if we can carefully choose our brunch spot based on the mimosas and avocado toast, we should definitely scrutinize who's running a company!

5. From Dollar Store to Dior: Decoding Price Points and Profits

Let's talk about the price tags on your company's products. Are they budget-friendly, like the dollar store? Mid-range, like your everyday retail brands? Or do they fall into the luxury category, like the coveted shelves of Louis Vuitton or Dior? Understanding where your company's products fit into the price spectrum is key because it attracts different types of clientele.

- **Low-Price Products:** Companies with lower-priced products cater to a broad customer base looking for affordability and value. Think of discount stores where shoppers appreciate deals. While this can mean high sales volume, the profit margins are often slimmer. These businesses need to operate with razor-thin margins and high efficiency to stay profitable. However, they may struggle to bounce back during tough economic times due to their lower profit per item.
- **Mid-Range Products:** Companies in the mid-range price bracket strike a

balance between affordability and quality. They attract a steady stream of customers looking for decent quality without breaking the bank. This category applies to the majority of businesses, making it highly competitive. The abundance of competition means these companies must continuously innovate and improve to stand out. While mid-range companies still have to watch their margins, they may fare better during economic downturns compared to budget brands.

- **Luxury Products:** On the other end of the spectrum, luxury brands offer premium products with high price tags. Shoppers at Louis Vuitton, for instance, aren't as fazed when prices increase by $200 or more for their favorite arm candy. Luxury brands benefit from high profit margins per item, which can contribute to substantial profitability. However, their customer base is smaller, requiring the brand to appeal strongly to a niche market. The special status and high reputation of luxury brands can help them keep loyal customers, even when the economy is unstable.

Understanding where a company fits in the pricing scale helps you see its market strategy and strength. Luxury brands focus on being exclusive and having high profit margins, while budget brands depend on selling a lot of products quickly and efficiently. Mid-range companies try to balance low prices and good quality, competing in a busy market.

Exploring the world of competitive advantage in pricing is like hunting for buried treasure. Imagine your company as a savvy pirate ship, navigating through choppy economic waters. High profit margins are your golden coins, making your ship more resilient during financial storms. These precious profits allow you to reinvest in exciting growth opportunities, like upgrading your ship or expanding your fleet. Companies with high profit margins are the seasoned pirates of the business world, expertly controlling costs and staying ahead of the competition. So, ensure your pricing strategy is spot-on, and your company will sail smoothly, even when the seas get rough!

In short, whether a company caters to bargain hunters or high-end shoppers, its pricing strategy greatly impacts its business model and market stability. So, where does your company fit in, and how does its pricing strategy affect its market performance?

Companies that have a competitive edge typically possess strong pricing power. These are companies that can maintain or raise prices without losing customers. Such companies usually have a distinct advantage because their products or services are perceived as unique or essential, allowing them to avoid price wars and protect their profit margins. This pricing power is often found in brands with high customer loyalty, unique products, or dominant market positions. So, take a look at your list of companies. Does each company have a competitive advantage?

A strong company doesn't need to tick every single box, like high profit margins, effective management, a killer brand identity, multiple income streams, or unique patents and processes. But the more boxes they check, the better their standing. Personally, I like to see at least three boxes checked - it's a solid benchmark for spotting a potentially strong investment. After all, even the best pizza needs more than just dough to be delicious. So, aim for those extra toppings to ensure your investment isn't just plain cheese!

Chapter 6

Diva of Due Diligence: Navigating Stock Research Like a Queen

This is where you, the savvy Investor, stand apart from the wild speculator!

Let's break it down: Investment vs. Speculation. Investing means you're all about thorough analysis, safeguarding your principal, and aiming for a decent return. You're like a financial Sherlock Holmes, uncovering the best opportunities with careful consideration. Speculation, on the other hand, is like betting on a horse race – it's all about potential price movements and comes with a hefty dose of risk.

Now, it's your turn to shine and transform your life. Step into the spotlight as a wise investor, not a reckless speculator. Let's make those smart moves and turn your financial dreams into reality!

You've identified some dazzling companies with high returns and a sparkling competitive advantage, it's time to elevate our analysis. Instead of stopping at the surface, let's dive deeper into their financial statements and examine the fundamental metrics that define winning companies. Welcome to the world of Fundamental Analysis – the bedrock of smart investing!

Financial Statements: The Secret Diary of a Company

Think of financial statements as the company's diary, but instead of juicy secrets and love confessions, you get numbers and financial drama. These documents tell the story of a company's financial highs and lows over a specific period, typically on a quarterly or annual basis.

As an investor, financial statements are essential because they offer a transparent view of a company's financial health. Want to know if that company is worth your hard-earned cash? These statements are your crystal ball, showing you if the company is thriving, barely surviving, or somewhere in between. It's all about making sure you're not investing in the financial equivalent of a trendy gadget that breaks after a week.

Financial statements serve multiple purposes. First, they're crucial for decision-making, providing vital information for investment, lending, and management choices. Second, they act as a performance measurement tool, allowing investors and management to see how the company's doing compared to its goals and industry benchmarks – it's like checking the company's diary to see if it kept its New Year's resolutions. Third, they offer transparency, showing, "Hey, this company has nothing to hide," unlike that one ex who was always "busy." Lastly, public companies are legally required to disclose their financials, making it a mandatory open-diary policy – you get to read everything upfront.
Financial statements typically include:

- **Balance Sheet:** This statement offers an overview of the company's assets, liabilities, and shareholders' equity at a specific moment. It shows what the company owns and owes. Think of it as the company's financial face without any filters.
- **Income Statement (Profit and Loss Statement):** This is the juicy part that shows the company's money earned, costs, and overall profits or losses for a certain time. It's like finding out if the company is dining on caviar or surviving on instant noodles.
- **Cash Flow Statement:** This statement tracks where the company's money is coming from and where it's going (cash inflows and outflows) over a period. It shows how well the company manages its cash position, covering operating, investing, and financing activities. It's like tracking your shopping sprees and savings.
- **Statement of Changes in Equity:** This statement shows how the company's equity changed during the reporting period, such as profits or losses, dividends paid, and other adjustments. It's the drama in the shareholders' world – who got richer, who cashed out, and who stayed the course.

You can uncover a company's financial statements in several spots. First, check out the company's website, where most publicly traded firms post them in the investor relations section. The Securities and Exchange Commission (SEC) in the U.S. requires companies to file their financials in the EDGAR database at www.sec.gov. Annual reports (also known as 10-K) are like the company's yearbook, packed with all the detailed financials, management gossip, and sneak peeks at future plans – a real treasure trove of information. While companies also release quarterly statements, those can be a bit like summer flings: fun and exciting but not always the full picture. Because companies can have seasonal products that do better at certain times of the year, we focus on annual statements to get a clear view of their overall performance.

Financial documents are packed with terms that can make your head spin, let's focus on the ones we need to tackle first.

Revenue: Revenue is the total amount of money a company earns from selling its goods or services. It's like the income you get from your job, but for a business, it comes from selling products or providing services to customers. Revenue is often called "sales" or "top-line income" because it's the first line you see on an income statement.

For example, if you own a boutique and sell $10,000 worth of dresses in a month, that $10,000 is your revenue. It doesn't matter yet what it costs you to make those dresses or pay your staff—revenue just shows the total money coming in from sales.

Understanding revenue is crucial because it shows how well a company is rocking its core business activities. Higher revenue usually means the business is selling more products or services, a fantastic sign of growth and success. When we check out company financials, we want to see that revenue line climbing year after year, like a hit song on the charts.

Revenue Growth: Revenue Growth is all about how much more money a company is making compared to before. It's usually measured as a percentage. For example, if a company made $1 million last year and $1.2 million this year, you'd calculate the revenue growth like this:

Formula:

$$\text{Revenue Growth Percentage} = \left(\frac{R_{current} - R_{previous}}{R_{previous}}\right) \times 100$$

$$\text{Revenue Growth Percentage} = \left(\frac{\$1,200,000 - \$1,000,000}{\$1,000,000}\right) \times 100$$

$$\text{Revenue Growth Percentage} = 20\%$$

The company's revenue growth rate would be 20%. If a company's revenue keeps going up like this, it means the business is growing and doing well. On the other hand, if the revenue isn't growing, it might be a sign that something needs fixing. By looking at revenue growth, companies can see what's working, what's not, and plan for the future. It's like having a map that shows you where the treasure is buried – essential for keeping the business booming!

Net Income: Net income, also known as net profit or net earnings, is the total profit a company makes after subtracting all its expenses from its total revenue. These expenses include the cost of goods sold (COGS), operating expenses (like rent, utilities, and salaries), interest, and taxes. Net income is frequently referred to as the "bottom line" since it's the final line on an income statement and shows the company's overall profitability.

For example, if your boutique rakes in $10,000 in revenue, has $4,000 in COGS, $3,000 in operating expenses, and $500 in taxes, your net income would be calculated like this:

Formula:

Net Income = Total Revenue − COGS − Operating Expenses − Taxes

Net Income = $10,000 − $4,000 − $3,000 − $500

Net Income = $2,500

Net income is essential because it shows the actual profit your business has made during a specific period. It's like the finishing touch on your financial sundae, showing the company's financial health and its ability to generate profit after covering all its costs. Investors, analysts, and business owners closely monitor net income to make informed decisions about the company's financial strategies and future development. Just like revenue, we want to see net income increase year after year to show growth. If this doesn't happen, we need to find out why and determine if it's due to investments that will bring future profit or rising costs. So, keep an eye on that bottom line and watch your business thrive!

Net Income Growth: Net Income Growth is like tracking how much more profit the company is making compared to before. It's usually measured as a percentage, showing the increase (or decrease) in net income over a specific period, such as year-over-year (YoY). For instance, suppose a company earned a net income of $1 million in the previous year and $1.5 million this year. The calculation would be:

Formula:

$$\text{Net Income Growth Rate (\%)} = \left(\frac{NIcurrent - NIprevious}{NIprevious}\right) \times 100$$

$$\text{Net Income Growth Rate (\%)} = \left(\frac{\$1,500,000 - \$1,000,000}{\$1,000,000}\right) \times 100$$

Net Income Growth Rate (%) = 50%

Therefore, the company's net income growth rate would be 50%. If net income keeps increasing, it's a great sign that the company is getting more efficient and profitable. By tracking net income growth, you can see if the company's profits are on the rise, like watching your savings grow in a piggy bank. It's a key indicator of financial health and future potential, keeping investors excited and the company thriving!

Net Profit Margin: To get a clearer picture of a company's profitability and efficiency, we look at the ratio of net earnings to total revenue. This ratio is often referred to as the net profit margin. It tells us what percentage of the total revenue remains as net profit after all expenses, including operating costs, interest, taxes, and other expenses, have been deducted.

If a company is showing a net profit margin of over 20%, it's like they've got a secret sauce – a competitive advantage that sets them apart from the rest. It means they're not just bringing in a lot of money; they're also keeping a good chunk of it as profit. This indicates efficiency, strong management, and a solid market position.

For example, imagine a lemonade stand run by a savvy kid named Bob. If Bob makes $1.00 from selling lemonade and keeps 20 cents after buying lemons, sugar, and cups, paying his little sister a marketing fee, and giving a nickel to the tax man, Bob's net profit margin is 20%. He's basically the Warren Buffett of Lemonade!

In short, a high net profit margin is a sign that a company knows how to turn its hard-earned revenue into solid profits, making it a potential star performer in the business world.

Let's say a company has a total revenue of $1,000,000 and a net income of $250,000 for a year.

Formula:

$$\text{Net Profit Margin} = \left(\frac{\text{Net Income}}{\text{Total Revenue}}\right) \times 100$$

$$\text{Net Profit Margin} = \left(\frac{\$250,000}{\$1,000,000}\right) \times 100$$

$$\text{Net Profit Margin} = 25\%$$

In this example, the company has a net profit margin of 25%, which indicates a strong competitive advantage. It means that for every dollar of revenue, the company keeps 25 cents as profit after covering all its expenses.

While less than 20% net profit margins might be a cause for scrutiny, it's not necessarily bad; it needs to be assessed in the context of the industry norms, business model, strategic goals, and operational efficiency of the company.

Here are the standard net profit margins considered outstanding or very good for various sectors or industries, indicating a competitive edge:

Technology: 20% and above

Healthcare and Pharmaceuticals: 15% and above

Financial Services: 15% and above

Consumer Goods (Non-Discretionary), also known as Consumer Staples: 10% and above

Consumer Goods (Discretionary): 8% and above

Retail: 5% and above

Energy: 10% and above

Utilities: 8% and above

Telecommunications: 10% and above

Real Estate: 15% and above

Industrial Manufacturing: 10% and above
Transportation and Logistics: 8% and above
Media and Entertainment: 12% and above
Hospitality and Tourism: 10% and above
Agriculture and Food Production: 5% and above
These benchmarks can vary based on specific market conditions, economic cycles, and geographic regions. However, achieving these net profit margins generally indicates that a company is operating efficiently and has a competitive advantage in its industry.

Cost of Goods Sold (COGS): Cost of Goods Sold (COGS) is the grand total of what it takes to produce the fabulous goods or services a company sells. Think of it as the behind-the-scenes cost of creating the magic! This includes expenses for raw materials, labor, and any other costs directly tied to making those products. COGS is essential because it tells us how much it really costs to bring those items to life.

For example, if your chic boutique spends $4,000 to make dresses and sells them for $10,000, the COGS is $4,000. That means the money left over from sales, after covering the production cost, is $6,000. This leftover cash is called gross profit — a.k.a. the sweet spot! Understanding COGS helps businesses figure out their production costs and set prices that ensure they stay in the green.

Gross Profit: Gross profit is the money a company makes from selling its products or services after subtracting the direct costs associated with producing them (COGS). It's the shining number that shows how much a company earns from its main activities before we even think about other expenses like rent, utilities, and salaries. To find this fabulous figure, just subtract the COGS from the total revenue. Voilà, you've got your gross profit — a clear indicator of your business's core earning power!

Formula:

Gross Profit = Total Revenue − Cost of Goods Sold (COGS)

Gross profit is your company's way of showing off how well it's producing and selling its products. A higher gross profit means the company is acing it at keeping production costs low and pricing products perfectly.

Gross Profit Margin: Gross profit margin is a percentage that shows how much of each dollar of revenue is kept as gross profit after accounting for the Cost of Goods Sold (COGS). It indicates the proportion of revenue that exceeds the COGS and measures a company's profitability relative to its revenue. As a general rule (with some exceptions), companies with gross profit margins above the industry benchmarks tend to have a higher competitive edge. They retain more money from each dollar earned after covering the cost of goods sold. This extra profit allows them to invest in marketing, research, and product improvement, helping them grow and stay ahead of competitors. Additionally, higher margins provide a financial cushion to absorb unexpected costs or market downturns, contributing to their overall stability and resilience.

Companies with gross profit margins under these benchmarks are often in highly competitive industries where it's tough to stay afloat. They often struggle because they keep less money from each dollar earned. This limits their ability to spend on essential activities like marketing and product development, making it harder to attract and retain customers. Furthermore, industries with low margins typically have intense competition, which forces companies to keep prices low and further squeezes their profits.

Here are the standard gross profit margins considered outstanding for various sectors or industries, indicating a competitive edge:

Technology: 60% and above

Healthcare and Pharmaceuticals: 60% and above

Financial Services: 50% and above

Consumer Goods (Non-Discretionary), also known as Consumer Staples: 40% and above

Consumer Goods (Discretionary): 40% and above

Retail: 30% and above

Energy: 30% and above

Utilities: 40% and above

Telecommunications: 60% and above

Real Estate: 50% and above

Industrial Manufacturing: 35% and above

Transportation and Logistics: 30% and above

Media and Entertainment: 60% and above

Hospitality and Tourism: 40% and above

Agriculture and Food Production: 25% and above

Ready to crunch some numbers? Here's the calculation to figure out your gross profit margins on this example: If your boutique's gross profit is $6,000 and your total revenue is $10,000, what would your gross profit margin be?

Formula:

$$\text{Gross Profit Margin} = \left(\frac{\text{Gross Profit}}{\text{Total Revenue}}\right) \times 100$$

$$\text{Gross Profit Margin} = \left(\frac{\$6,000}{\$10,000}\right) \times 100$$

$$\text{Gross Profit Margin} = 60\%$$

Understanding and managing your gross profit margin is key to staying competitive and profitable in your industry.

To summarize, the difference between net profit margin and gross profit margin lies in what costs are deducted from revenue to calculate each margin, and what each margin ultimately represents about a company's profitability.

Key Differences:

Cost Deduction:

- Gross Profit Margin only deducts the cost of goods sold.
- Net Profit Margin deducts all expenses, including operating costs, interest, and taxes.

Purpose:

- Gross Profit Margin indicates how efficiently a company produces and sells its goods.
- Net Profit Margin provides a complete picture of overall profitability after all expenses.

Financial Insight:

- Gross Profit Margin helps assess production efficiency and cost management.
- Net Profit Margin helps assess the overall financial health and profitability of the company.

In essence, while gross profit margin focuses on production-related profitability, net profit margin gives a broader view of the company's financial performance, considering all aspects of its operations.

By analyzing year-over-year growth in revenue, net income, net profit margins and gross profit margins, you can gain insights into a company's performance. For the full scoop, you should dive into a company's financial statements over at least 5-10 years. Think of it as binge-watching a TV series to catch all the plot twists and character development! This long-term view helps uncover trends in revenue, net income, net profit margins and gross profit margins. If these numbers are consistently rising, it's like the company has nailed the season finale—showing it's well-managed, financially fit, and ready to reward its loyal fans, a.k.a. investors, with some sweet returns.

You'll also be able to spot turning points. Just like realizing your favorite character isn't the hero you thought they were, you might find that a company on an upward trajectory is suddenly missing the mark—think Nokia when Apple entered the scene or Toys 'R' Us when Amazon grew in popularity. If you notice profits and income not growing over 2-3 years or a clear downward movement during this period, it's like spotting a plot twist that screams "Time to move on!"

Some companies' financial statements are easier to read than others. I like to stay away from those that make it overly complicated. This can be a sign that they're either trying to hide something or they need to hire someone new to clearly spill the beans on their numbers.

Ensure the data you are comparing is consistent year-over-year. Any changes in accounting methods or restatements should be noted. The companies we are going to look at do include these details, but for this example, I left them out to keep it simple. Also, keep in mind the impact of inflation to get a real sense of growth. Economic conditions, industry trends, and company-specific events can all impact financial results.

Let's do some exercises and see if you can spot the difference. Here are two tables with company revenue, net income, net profit margins and gross profit margins.

NVIDIA Corporation (NVDA)

Fiscal Year	Revenue in Million USD	Net Income in Million USD	Net Profit Margins (%)	Gross Profit Margins (%)
2024	60,922	29,760	48.85	72.72
2023	26,974	4,368	16.19	56.93
2022	26,914	9,752	36.23	64.93
2021	16,675	4,332	25.98	62.34
2020	10,918	2,796	25.61	61.99
2019	11,716	4,141	35.34	61.21
2018	9,714	3,047	31.37	59.93
2017	6,910	1,666	24.11	58.80
2016	5,010	614	12.26	56.11
2015	4,682	631	13.48	55.51

Nvidia, the tech wizard behind cutting-edge GPUs and AI technology, hit a few speed bumps during their 2020 fiscal year thanks to the COVID-19 pandemic. With supply chains in a tangle and economic activities on pause, businesses and consumers tightened their wallets, leading to a drop in sales. The pandemic's shockwaves caused market volatility and uncertainty, especially in the tech sector, making investors jittery and people hesitant to splurge on new gadgets.

Fast forward to fiscal 2023, Nvidia's revenue held steady at $26.97 billion, just a smidge above the $26.91 billion from 2022. But the fourth quarter took a nosedive, with revenue dropping 21% to $6.05 billion from $7.64 billion the previous year. On top of that, their operating expenses soared to $11.13 billion from $7.43 billion in fiscal 2022, thanks to hefty investments in research and development and a whopping $1.35 billion hit from ditching an acquisition. Nvidia's financial journey was also rocked by broader market issues, like a dip in demand for GPUs in gaming and professional visualization, plus the added headaches of inflation and geopolitical tensions.

Despite a hiccup in the last quarter of 2023, Nvidia shows consistent growth across all fields, with net margins exceeding 20% for 7 out of the last 10 years, and gross profit margins shot up to 70.72% in the last fiscal year.
Now, if the 2024 fiscal year had shown a downward trend in all these areas, caution would be in order. That's why it's crucial to look beyond just stock charts. Reviewing net profit margins is like making sure your high heels have enough cushioning—you need that extra support to keep things comfortable and steady.

E.l.f. Beauty, Inc. (ELF)

Fiscal Year	Revenue in Million USD	Net Income in Million USD (loss)	Net Profit Margins (%)	Gross Profit Margins (%)
2024	1,023,932	127,663	12.47	70.72
2023	578,844	61,530	10.63	67.44
2022	392,155	21,770	5.55	64.19
2021	318,110	6,232	1.96	64.82
2020	282,851	17,884	6.32	64.03
2019*	66,141	(17,914)	-27.08	61.22
2018	267,435	15,525	5.81	60.85
2017	269,888	33,475	12.40	61.03
2016	229,567	5,313	2.31	57.60

*Three months ended March 31, 2019 (transition period)
E.l.f. Cosmetics, operating as e.l.f. Beauty, entered the stock market on September 22, 2016.

E.l.f. Beauty, Inc. known for its affordable and trendy cosmetics, faced some profit challenges in recent years. The profit decline in 2018 was mainly due to a big jump in operating expenses. They spent more on marketing, formed new retail partnerships, and paid restructuring costs to streamline operations and set the stage for future growth.

In fiscal year 2019, e.l.f. Beauty saw profits drop again, this time due to increased competition and higher costs from launching new products and running marketing campaigns. The company was also feeling the effects of strategic changes, like closing underperforming stores and shifting focus to online sales.

By fiscal year 2020, the costs kept climbing as e.l.f. Beauty expanded its digital marketing and e-commerce efforts. On top of that, the COVID-19 pandemic drove up shipping and logistics expenses. While these investments were crucial for maintaining growth, they took a toll on short-term profitability. Despite these challenges, e.l.f. Beauty remains committed to its mission of providing affordable beauty products.

E.l.f. Beauty, a standout in the Consumer Staples sector, consistently flaunts impressive gross profit margins above the 40% benchmark. However, they've only achieved net profit margins of 10% and above in the past two years, signaling a promising upward trend. This improvement suggests that the company is becoming more efficient at managing its operating expenses and finding ways to increase profitability. It's a positive sign that e.l.f. Beauty is adapting and optimizing its strategies to enhance its bottom line.

Without diving too deep into the details, let's explore some possible reasons for the low performance in net profit margins:

High Operating Expenses: Even if the gross profit margin is high, high operating expenses (such as marketing, salaries, rent, and administrative costs) can eat into the net profit. If a company spends a lot on advertising, branding, and expanding their market presence, these costs can significantly reduce net profit margins.

Interest Expenses: If a company has significant debt, the interest payments on that debt can lower net profit margins. This means a portion of their revenue is going towards paying interest rather than contributing to net profit.

High Tax Rates: High taxes can also impact net profit margins. If the company operates in regions with high corporate taxes, a substantial portion of their profit might be going towards tax payments.

Investment in Growth: A company might be reinvesting a lot of their revenue into growth initiatives such as opening new stores, developing new product lines, or expanding into new markets. These investments can increase expenses in the short term, leading to lower net profit margins.

Non-operational Costs: Costs such as restructuring charges, write-offs, or one-time expenses can also impact net profit margins. These are not regular operational costs but can significantly affect the net profit in the period they are incurred.

All of these details can be found in their financial statements.

While some of these indicators are promising for the company's development, others raise concerns. Investing in growth, such as opening new stores or launching innovative products, shows future planning and can boost long-term revenues. Conversely, high-interest payments and frequent non-operational costs are red flags, indicating potential financial strain and poor management. High operating expenses can be good if they're tied to strategic initiatives like marketing, but high taxes need context — they could mean the company is profitable despite operating in high-tax areas.

It's just like dating: a person who invests in themselves and has a clear plan for the future is a keeper. But if they're always borrowing money and dealing with unexpected "one-time" expenses, it might be time to reconsider!

Congratulations, you just unlocked the secret code to spot if a company is truly growing or just pretending! It's all in the numbers. First, check out the revenue - are they making more money than last year? Next up, net income – are they actually keeping some of that cash after expenses, or is it vanishing into a black hole? Then there's the net profit margins and gross profit margins – think of these as the company's money-making muscles. The bigger, the better! If a company's flexing all these metrics in the right direction, it's not just surviving, it's thriving.

These are the basic calculations you should look out for, and therefore you can jump right to Chapter 7. But if you want to get really fancy, there are even more financial terms and metrics to explore.:

Operating Expenses: Operating expenses are the costs a company sustains to keep the daily gears turning smoothly. These include expenses like rent for office space, salaries for employees, utility bills, marketing costs, and supplies. Unlike the cost of goods sold (COGS), which are the direct costs of producing goods, operating expenses cover all the other costs necessary to keep the business humming.

For example, if you own a boutique, your operating expenses would include the rent for your fabulous shop, the salaries of your stylish staff, the electricity bills to keep the lights sparkling, and the cost of advertising your latest collection. These expenses are crucial because they allow your business to function like a well-oiled machine every day.

Assets: Assets are everything a company owns that has value and can be used to meet its obligations, generate income, and support its operations. They are resources that can provide future economic benefits. Assets are generally divided into two primary categories: current assets and non-current assets.

- **Current Assets:** Assets that can be easily converted into cash within one year. Examples include cash itself, accounts receivable (money owed by customers), and inventory (goods available for sale). For instance, if your boutique has

$5,000 in cash, $3,000 in inventory, and $2,000 in accounts receivable, these are your current assets.

- **Non-Current Assets:** These are long-term assets that are not anticipated to be turned into cash within a year. Examples include property, equipment, and vehicles. For example, if your boutique owns the building it operates in or has equipment used to create the dresses, these are non-current assets.

Understanding assets is crucial for assessing a company's financial health. They represent the resources available to a business for growth, operations, and investment. By effectively managing and utilizing assets, a company can ensure its long-term success and stability. Think of assets as the company's secret stash of chocolate – properly managed, they'll keep the business energized and thriving, even on the toughest days!

Liabilities: Liabilities are the amounts of money that a company owes to others. They represent financial obligations like loans, bills, and other debts that need to be paid in the future. While they are a part of a company's financial picture, we actually want to see fewer liabilities. Why? Because too many debts that banks could call in at any moment might push a company into financial trouble. Think of liabilities as the pesky weeds in a garden – the fewer, the better for a healthy, flourishing business!

- **Current Liabilities:** These are debts or obligations that need to be paid within one year. Examples include accounts payable (money the company owes to suppliers), short-term loans, and taxes owed. For instance, if your boutique owes $2,000 to a fabric supplier and $1,000 in short-term loans, these are your current liabilities.

- **Non-Current Liabilities:** These are long-term debts or obligations that are not due within one year. Examples include long-term loans and mortgages. For example, if your boutique has a $50,000 loan that will be paid off over several years, this is a non-current liability.

Understanding liabilities is key to gauging a company's financial stability and its capacity to meet financial obligations. By managing liabilities effectively, a company ensures it has enough resources to pay its debts while still investing in growth and operations. Just like our personal debt can put a dent in our wallets, excessive company debt can cause big headaches when the market shifts or if banks demand repayment all at once. A good rule of thumb? Debt should be manageable enough to pay back within 3-4 years with their profits. If they can't swing that, they might not be the best bet.

Equity (Shareholders' Equity): Equity, also known as shareholders' equity, is the portion of a company's assets that belongs to the owners or shareholders after all liabilities have been paid off. It represents the net value of the company and can be thought of as the owners' claim on the business assets.

To understand equity, consider it as what's left when you subtract all the money a company owes (liabilities) from everything it owns (assets). For example, if your boutique has $100,000 in assets (like cash, inventory, and equipment) and $60,000 in liabilities (like loans and bills), the equity would be $40,000. This $40,000 is the value that belongs to the owners or shareholders.

Equity is like the financial health report card for a company. Positive equity means the company has more assets than liabilities, giving it an A+ for financial strength. Negative equity, on the other hand, is like getting a big, red F – it means liabilities are outweighing assets and there's trouble on the horizon. For investors and owners, equity represents their slice of the company pie and the potential for some sweet returns. So, think of equity as your golden ticket to understanding just how robust a company's finances are – and whether it's heading for the honor roll or detention!

Debt-to-Equity Ratio: Think of the Debt-to-Equity Ratio as the financial seesaw balancing act between what a company owes and what it owns. The Debt-to-Equity Ratio measures how much debt a company uses to finance its operations compared to its equity.

To keep it simple, if a company has a high Debt-to-Equity Ratio, it means they're relying more on borrowed money (debt) than on their own funds (equity). This can be risky, like trying to balance a teeter-totter with a sumo wrestler on one end and a feather on the other! On the flip side, a lower ratio suggests a more conservative approach, using more of its own money to fuel growth. This ratio aids investors in assessing a company's financial leverage and risk profile.

To calculate the debt-to-equity ratio, you divide the total debt by the total equity. For instance, if your boutique has $60,000 in debt (loans and bills) and $40,000 in equity (the net value of the company), the debt-to-equity ratio would be:

Formula:

$$\text{Debt-to-Equity Ratio} = \frac{\text{Total Liabilities}}{\text{Shareholders' Equity}}$$

$$\text{Debt-to-Equity Ratio} = \frac{\$60,000}{\$40,000}$$

$$\text{Debt-to-Equity Ratio} = 1.5$$

This means that for every dollar of equity, the company has $1.50 in debt. Therefore, a company with low or no debt-to-equity ratios has a leg up over those with higher ratios. A strong balance sheet with minimal debt is like having an umbrella on a rainy day—it helps the company better weather economic storms and stay financially stable. Short-term debt is particularly tricky; it's like having a demanding friend who always wants their money back quickly, which can be a real strain during economic slumps or tight credit conditions.

To achieve the best returns, focusing on long-term performance is key. High debt levels can be like trying to run a marathon with a heavy backpack; it hinders a company's ability to grow and create value over time. By keeping debt levels low, companies can more effectively align with long-term investment goals. Plus, companies that operate efficiently and generate strong cash flow can fund their growth and operations without relying heavily on debt, leading to those enviably low debt-to-equity ratios.

Return on Equity (ROE): While we're on the subject of Equity, let's talk about Return on Equity (ROE), the superstar of financial metrics! ROE evaluates how efficiently a company utilizes its equity to produce profits.

Think of it as the ultimate performance review for a company, showing how well it's turning shareholders' investments into earnings.

Think of ROE as the "bang for your buck" metric. If you invest in a company, you want to know how much profit they're generating with your money. A higher ROE means the company is doing a fantastic job of squeezing the most profit out of every dollar of equity. It's like having a magical kitchen where every ingredient you throw in, turns into a gourmet dish!

To calculate ROE, you use this simple formula:

$$\text{ROE (\%)} = \left(\frac{\text{Net Income}}{\text{Shareholders Equity}}\right) \times 100$$

For instance, if a company reports a net income of $2 million and has shareholders' equity totaling $10 million, the return on equity (ROE) would be 20%. This means the company generated 20 cents of profit for every dollar of equity. Pretty neat, right?

$$\text{ROE (\%)} = \left(\frac{\$2,000,000}{\$10,000,000}\right) \times 100$$

$$\text{ROE} = 20\%$$

In summary, ROE gives investors a quick look at how effectively a company is using their investment to generate earnings. It's like a superhero power, revealing the financial strength and efficiency of a company with just one number. So, next time you're evaluating a company, don't forget to check out their ROE and see just how super their financial performance is!

Cash Flow from Operating Activities: This refers to the money a company generates or spends as a result of its regular business operations. It includes all cash transactions related to the company's core activities, such as selling products, providing services, paying suppliers, and covering operating expenses like rent and salaries.

For example, if your boutique sells $10,000 worth of dresses, pays $4,000 for materials and labor, and spends $2,000 on rent and utilities, the cash flow from operating activities would be the net cash generated from these transactions. In this case, it would be $10,000 (cash inflows) minus $6,000 (cash outflows), resulting in a positive cash flow of $4,000.

Formula:

Positive Cash Flow = Sales − Materials and Labor − Rent and Utilities

Positive Cash Flow = $10,000 − $4,000 − $2,000

Positive Cash Flow = $4,000

Understanding cash flow from operating activities is crucial because it tells you how much cash a company is raking in from its day-to-day business. This helps you see if the company can keep things running, pay its bills, and invest in its future. If the cash flow is positive, it means the company is making enough money to cover its expenses and keep things humming. But if it's negative, it might be a sign that the company is in a bit of a financial pickle.

To get the complete picture, you also include non-cash expenses (like depreciation and amortization) and changes in working capital in the calculation:

$$
\begin{array}{rl}
 & \text{Net Income} \\
+ & \text{Depreciation} \\
+ & \text{Amortization} \\
+ & \text{Changes in Working Capital} \\
+ & \underline{\text{Other Non-Cash Items}} \\
 & \text{Cash Flow from Operating Activities}
\end{array}
$$

This full formula helps to adjust the net income for non-cash items and changes in working capital, providing a clearer picture of the actual cash generated by a company's operating activities.

Earnings per Share and Diluted Earnings per Share: Let's dive into the essentials of Basic EPS and Diluted EPS, and understand why Diluted EPS is often considered the more insightful metric.

Basic EPS (Earnings Per Share) is a straightforward measure of a company's profitability on a per-share basis. It's calculated by dividing the company's net income by the number of shares currently outstanding. This gives you a snapshot of how much profit each share of stock is earning.

Basic EPS Formula:

$$
\text{Basic EPS} = \frac{\text{Net Income}}{\text{Number of Outstanding Shares}}
$$

Think of Basic EPS as counting the confirmed guests at a dinner party. It tells you how much profit is allocated to each existing share.

However, companies often have potential shares that could be created through stock options, warrants, or convertible securities. These potential shares are like guests who might join the party later. This is where Diluted EPS comes in.

Diluted EPS (Earnings Per Share) takes into account all possible shares that could be issued. It's calculated by dividing the net income by the total number of shares, including both current and potential shares. This gives a more comprehensive view of the company's earnings per share.

Diluted EPS Formula:

$$\text{Diluted EPS} = \frac{\text{Net Income}}{\text{Total Potential Shares}}$$

Why is Diluted EPS often considered a better metric? It provides a more realistic and conservative view of a company's profitability. By accounting for all potential shares, Diluted EPS prepares investors for the full scope of possible share dilution, offering a clearer picture of the company's financial health.

To illustrate, imagine a company's profit as a pie. Basic EPS shows you how the pie is divided among the current shareholders. Diluted EPS, on the other hand, considers everyone who might get a slice if more shares are issued. This way, you're better prepared to understand the true value and potential earnings per share.

In summary, while Basic EPS provides a quick snapshot, Diluted EPS gives a more complete and prudent assessment of a company's profitability. It's the preferred metric for investors looking to make informed decisions about the company's financial performance and future growth.

Price to Earnings (P/E) Ratio: This is a measurement that compares a company's present stock price to its earnings per share (EPS). It tells you how much investors are willing to pay today for a dollar of the company's earnings.

P/E Ratio Formula:

$$\text{P/E Ratio} = \frac{\text{Market Price per Share}}{\text{Earnings per Share (EPS)}}$$

For instance, let's assume a company's stock is priced at $100 per share and the EPS is $5, the P/E ratio would be:

$$\text{P/E Ratio} = \frac{\$100}{\$5}$$

P/E Ratio = 20

This indicates that investors are prepared to pay $20 for each $1 of earnings. The P/E ratio helps investors determine whether a stock is overvalued, undervalued, or fairly valued. Here's a deeper dive:

- **High P/E Ratio:** Indicates that investors expect higher earnings growth in the future, and are willing to pay a premium for the stock. It's like paying more for a brand-new gadget because you believe it has cutting-edge technology and great future potential.
- **Low P/E Ratio:** Suggests that the stock might be undervalued or that the company is facing challenges. It's akin to finding a good deal on a classic item that might have been overlooked.

However, the P/E ratio should be used in context. Comparing the P/E ratio to that of similar companies in the same industry or to the overall market can provide more insights. For example, tech companies typically have higher P/E ratios due to their growth potential, while utility companies might have lower P/E ratios because they are more stable and less growth-oriented.

If both companies are in the same industry, investors might consider them equally valued based on the P/E ratio. But if Company A is expected to grow earnings at 20% per year and Company B at 10%, investors might prefer Company A despite the same P/E ratio. It's like choosing between two equally priced cakes – you'd probably go for the one with double the frosting!

There isn't a specific number that defines a "high" or "low" P/E ratio because it varies by industry and market conditions. Here's how you can evaluate it:

- **Industry Comparison:** Compare the P/E ratio to other companies in the same industry. For example, a tech company with a P/E ratio of 20 might be considered low compared to its peers with ratios of 30 or higher.
- **Historical Comparison:** Look at the company's historical P/E ratios. If the current P/E is higher than its historical average, it might be overvalued, and if it's lower, it might be undervalued.
- **Market Comparison:** Compare the P/E ratio to the overall market average. For instance, if the average P/E ratio of the S&P 500 is 15 and a company's P/E is 25, it could be considered high.
- **Growth Expectations:** Consider the company's future earnings growth potential. A higher P/E ratio might be justified if the company is expected to grow significantly faster than its peers.

The P/E ratio is an essential tool for valuing stocks and making investment decisions, but it should be combined with other financial metrics and qualitative factors to obtain a comprehensive understanding of a company's valuation and growth prospects. Think of it as knowing how many sprinkles you get on your cupcake – the more context, the better!

Types of P/E Ratios

- **Trailing P/E:** Based on the past 12 months of earnings. It's like looking at a report card of what the company has already achieved.
- **Forward P/E:** Calculated using the estimated earnings for the upcoming 12 months. It's more like a sneak peek into the company's future potential.

Oof, that was a lot to take in all at once! But don't worry, there won't be a pop quiz at the end of this. These financial metrics are here to help you understand what you're looking at and to cut through the noise. Understanding and analyzing financial statements is like having a financial GPS for your investments. They help you make informed decisions, gauge how well a company is performing, and ensure everything is transparent and above board. Think of financial statements as your BFFs in the business world, always ready to spill the financial tea and guide you towards the smartest choices.

Chapter 7

Economic and Market Trends: Navigating Market Waves in Style

Trends come and go, just like flares and skinny jeans!

While our investment strategy goal is all about finding the 'McDreamy' of the stock market for those long-term, value-oriented vibes, dealing with market volatility can actually present some fantastic opportunities to snag quality stocks at a discount. Instead of letting it stress us out, we should focus on the real value of companies and keep our cool with patience and discipline. By seeing market ups and downs as chances to invest wisely and tuning out the short-term noise, we can build a strategy that's all about long-term growth and stability.

So, let's dive into how to spot economic and market trends!

The Economy and the Stock Market: A Dynamic Duo Explained

The economy and the stock market: Think of them as a dynamic duo, like Batman and Robin, but with more numbers and less crime-fighting. Let's break down how the economy works and how it affects the stock market, in a way that's easy to understand.

The economy is like the grand, interconnected network of all the creation, use, and exchange of services goods within a country (or the world). It's the giant, invisible machine that keeps everything running smoothly. Here's a simple way to think about it:

- **Production:** This is all about making things—cars, computers, cheeseburgers, you name it. Companies and factories produce goods and services.
- **Consumption:** This is us, the consumers, buying and using those goods and

75

services. Every time you buy a coffee, binge-watch a streaming series, or get a haircut, you're participating in the economy.

- **Trade:** This involves buying and selling between countries, like importing bananas from South America or exporting tech gadgets to Europe.

Key Components of the Economy

Gross Domestic Product (GDP): This is like the economy's report card. It measures the total value of all goods and services produced over a specific time period. A growing GDP generally means a healthy economy, while a shrinking GDP can indicate trouble.

Employment: High employment means more people have jobs, earn money, and spend money, which is good for the economy. High unemployment, on the other hand, can drag the economy down.

Inflation: This is the rate at which prices for goods and services increase. A little inflation is normal, usually between 2% and 4%, but too much can reduce your purchasing power. Imagine having to pay $10 for a loaf of bread—yikes! To ensure our investments grow in real terms, we need to earn a return that's higher than the inflation rate.

Interest Rates: Are set by central banks, like the Federal Reserve in the U.S. These rates influence how much it costs to borrow money. Lower interest rates mean it's cheaper to borrow money, which encourages people and businesses to spend and invest more.

How the Economy Affects the Stock Market

The stock market is like the economy's energetic little sibling. It's influenced by what's happening in the broader economy, and here's how:

Corporate Earnings: When the economy is doing well, companies generally experience higher sales and profits. This increased profitability makes their stocks more attractive to investors, which in turn drives up stock prices. For example, during a period of economic growth, a company like Apple might see a surge in sales of its iPhones and other products. As Apple reports higher earnings, investors become more interested in buying Apple's stock, which drives up the stock price.

Conversely, when the economy is struggling, companies often see lower sales and profits. This reduced profitability makes their stocks less appealing to investors, leading to falling stock prices. For instance, during a recession, consumer spending might decrease significantly, leading to lower sales for companies like Apple. If Apple reports lower earnings due to reduced sales, investors may become wary and start selling off their shares, causing the stock price to drop.

In summary, corporate earnings play a crucial role in influencing stock prices. Higher earnings during a strong economy attract investors and drive up stock prices, while lower earnings during economic downturns make stocks less attractive, leading to falling prices.

Consumer Confidence: The unemployment rate is an important factor in consumer confidence. When unemployment rates are low, more people have jobs and a steady income, which boosts their confidence and encourages them to spend more. This increased spending leads to higher profits for companies and, in turn, drives up stock prices.

When consumers feel confident about the economy, they are more likely to spend money. This increased spending boosts company profits and raises stock prices. For example, during a period of economic stability, consumers might feel secure in their jobs and financial situations, leading them to spend more on goods and services. Retailers like Amazon might see a significant increase in sales as people buy more products. As Amazon reports higher profits, investors become more interested in buying Amazon's stock, which drives up the stock price.

On the other hand, when unemployment rates are high, many people are out of work or worried about losing their jobs. This decreases consumer confidence and makes people spend less. Reduced spending can hurt company profits and drag down stock prices. For instance, during an economic downturn, consumers might be concerned about job security and future income, leading them to cut back on non-essential purchases. Retailers like Amazon might see a drop in sales as people become more cautious with their spending. If Amazon reports lower profits due to decreased consumer spending, investors may become wary and start selling off their shares, causing the stock price to fall.

Interest Rates: When interest rates are lower, borrowing money becomes cheaper. This means companies can finance expansions more easily, and consumers are more likely to take out loans for big purchases. We saw this firsthand during COVID-19 when interest rates dropped significantly. Many new homeowners took advantage of the low rates to purchase homes, while others refinanced their existing mortgages to secure lower interest rates. As a result, stock prices tended to rise.

Conversely, when interest rates are high, borrowing costs increase. This can slow down business investments and consumer spending. With high interest rates, people are less inclined to go on spending sprees, often leading to lower stock prices.

Inflation: Moderate inflation is a small increase in prices that usually indicates the economy is growing. This is generally good for stocks because it shows healthy economic activity.

However, high inflation can be a big problem. It makes things more expensive, reducing what people can buy, and often leads to higher interest rates, which can hurt stock prices.

For example, in the late 1970s and early 1980s, the United States faced very high inflation, with rates reaching up to 13.5% in 1980. This time, known as the Great Inflation, saw prices for goods and services rise quickly. To combat this, the Federal Reserve increased interest rates significantly, which slowed down economic growth and hurt stock prices.

Another example is more recent. In 2021 and 2022, many countries, including the United States, experienced high inflation due to supply chain issues, increased demand after COVID-19, and rising energy prices. The U.S. saw inflation rates go above 7% in 2021, the highest in nearly 40 years. This sharp rise in inflation led the Federal Reserve to consider raising interest rates to control it, causing concern among investors and making the stock market more volatile.

The highest inflation ever recorded occurred in Zimbabwe during the late 2000s. Zimbabwe experienced hyperinflation, where the inflation rate soared to unimaginable levels. In November 2008, Zimbabwe's monthly inflation rate reached an astronomical 79.6 billion percent, effectively rendering its currency worthless. At its peak, prices were doubling approximately every 24 hours.

This extreme case of hyperinflation was caused by a combination of economic mismanagement, political instability, and excessive money printing by the government in an attempt to address the economic crisis. Eventually, Zimbabwe abandoned its currency and began using foreign currencies like the U.S. dollar and South African rand to stabilize the economy.

Global Events: Positive events like trade deals, technological breakthroughs, and political stability can boost the economy and the stock market. For example, when countries sign beneficial trade deals, it can lead to more business activities and higher profits for companies, which in turn can drive up stock prices. Similarly, a new technological innovation, like the development of the internet or smartphones, can create new markets and opportunities, leading to increased stock prices for companies involved in that technology. Political stability also helps, as a stable government fosters economic growth and increases investor confidence.

On the other hand, negative events such as wars, natural disasters, and political instability can harm the economy and cause stock prices to fall. For instance, a war can disrupt trade and damage infrastructure, leading to economic downturns and falling stock prices. Natural disasters, like earthquakes or hurricanes, can cause serious damage to businesses and economies, resulting in declines in stock markets. Political instability, such as government upheavals or widespread protests, creates uncertainty and fear among investors, causing them to sell off stocks and driving prices down.

Knowing how the economy affects the stock market is important for making smart investment choices. But to really understand what's happening, you need to know about the different phases of economic cycles and how to analyze them. Economic cycles include periods when the economy is growing (expansion), slowing down (contraction), going through a tough time (recession), and bouncing back (recovery). These phases can affect how the stock market behaves and how investors feel.

Understanding these cycles can help you predict market changes, manage risks, and find opportunities. Economic cycles can last from a few months to several years, and spotting them early means looking at key indicators like GDP, job data, and inflation rates. By knowing these cycles and using the right analysis tools, you can better plan your investments and improve your chances of success.

Types of Economic Cycles

Expansion (Economic Growth): Expansion is a phase of the economic cycle where the economy grows, marked by increasing GDP, higher employment rates, and rising consumer and business spending. During this period, businesses expand, hire more workers, and consumers feel confident about their financial situations. Stock markets typically perform well during expansions as corporate earnings rise.

Contraction (Economic Slowdown): Contraction is the phase where the economy starts to slow down after a period of expansion. GDP growth slows or becomes negative, unemployment rates may rise, and consumer and business spending decreases. Stock markets may become volatile during this period, as investors anticipate lower corporate earnings.

Recession (Prolonged Contraction): A recession is a prolonged period of economic contraction lasting for at least two consecutive quarters. During a recession, GDP declines, unemployment rates increase significantly, and consumer and business spending drops. Stock markets often suffer during recessions as corporate earnings decline and investor confidence wanes.

Recovery (Post-Recession Growth): Recovery is the phase following a recession where the economy starts to grow again. GDP begins to rise, employment rates improve, and consumer and business spending increases. Stock markets typically start to recover during this period as investors anticipate better corporate earnings and improved economic conditions.

Think of the economy like the four seasons. Spring (expansion) is full of growth and new beginnings. Summer (contraction) is hot and sometimes too intense, causing things to slow down. Fall (recession) is when everything starts to wither and slow to a halt. Winter (recovery) is tough, but eventually, things start to thaw and bloom again. Watching the stock market through these cycles is like waiting for your favorite season to come around again.

Knowing how the economy affects the stock market is important for making smart investment choices. We've learned that economic factors like GDP, inflation, unemployment rates, and interest rates can impact stock prices. However, the stock market doesn't just react to these factors alone. It also follows broader patterns, called market trends, which show the overall direction and feeling in the market. To fully understand stock market movements, we need to look at these trends, such as bull and bear markets, which give us a clearer picture of how investors are behaving.

Bulls and Bears: The Wild Rollercoaster of Market Trends

Understanding economic markets and market trends is key to making smart investment decisions. Economic markets focus on big-picture indicators like GDP, inflation, and unemployment, which show the overall health of the economy. Market trends, on the other hand, deal with the behavior of stock prices over time, such as when the market is going up (bull market) or down (bear market). By learning about both, you can better predict changes, manage risks, and find opportunities.

Bull Markets: A bull market is a period where stock prices are rising or are expected to rise. This trend typically occurs when the economy is strong, with indicators like low unemployment, high consumer confidence, and robust corporate earnings. Investors are generally optimistic during bull markets, leading to increased buying and higher stock prices. For example, the stock market experienced a significant bull run during the 1990s, driven by technological advancements and strong economic growth. To remember this term, imagine your portfolio value getting thrown up into the air and reaching new astonishing heights that keep making you richer and richer.

Bear Market: Conversely, a bear market is a period where stock prices are falling or are expected to fall. Bear markets often happen during economic downturns, with indicators such as high unemployment, low consumer confidence, and declining corporate earnings. Investor sentiment is typically pessimistic, leading to selling and lower stock prices. A notable example is the bear market during the 2008 financial crisis, which was triggered by the housing market collapse and led to a severe economic recession. Think of it like watching your investments shrink and feeling like you've been mauled by a bear.

Sideways Trend (Flat Market): A flat market, also known as a sideways market, is characterized by a lack of significant movement in stock prices over a period of time. This trend occurs when stock prices don't move much in either direction for a period of time. This can happen when investors are unsure about the future, causing the market to stay steady. While it might seem boring, a flat market can be a good time to reassess and prepare for future opportunities.

A Quick Overview of the Characteristics and Indicators

Bull Markets:

- Rising stock prices
- High investor confidence
- Strong economic indicators (low unemployment, high GDP growth)
- Increased corporate earnings

Bear Markets:

- Falling stock prices
- Low investor confidence
- Weak economic indicators (high unemployment, negative GDP growth)
- Declining corporate earnings

Sideways Trend (Flat Market):

- Stable Prices Low Volatility
- Uncertain Investor Sentiment
- Consolidation Phase (The market is often in a consolidation phase, where previous gains or losses are digested before the next significant move.)
- Range-Bound Trading (Stocks trade within a defined range, often between a support level (bottom of the range) and a resistance level (top of the range).)

Knowing if the market is going up (bull phase) or down (bear phase) helps investors make smart choices. By watching economic signs and how investors feel, we can see these trends and change our plans if needed. This understanding is the first step to looking at market trends more closely, using tools to find patterns and predict what might happen next.

By explaining bull and bear markets early when discussing market trends, you give a strong base for understanding how the stock market moves. This method helps smoothly transition from the basic effects of the economy on stocks to the detailed specifics of market trends and what they mean for investors.

Understanding market trends, such as bull and bear markets, provides a solid foundation for recognizing the general direction of the stock market. However, to make more precise and informed investment decisions, it's essential to delve deeper into the tools and techniques used to analyze these trends. This is where technical analysis comes into play. By focusing on historical price movements, patterns, and various indicators, technical analysis allows investors to predict future price actions and identify potential trading opportunities. Let's explore how technical analysis can help you navigate the complexities of the market with greater accuracy and confidence.

Stock Market Detective: Cracking the Code with Technical Analysis

Technical analysis is a way to look at and predict the future prices of stocks by studying past price movements and trading activity. Unlike fundamental analysis, which looks at a company's financial health and business operations, technical analysis only focuses on the stock's past prices and trading volumes.

Imagine you're trying to predict if your favorite fashion brand will have a big sale soon. Instead of looking at the brand's financial reports or their store operations (like you would in fundamental analysis), you look at the past sale dates and patterns. You notice that every few months, the brand has a big sale. By recognizing this pattern, you can predict when the next sale might happen. Similarly, technical analysis uses past stock prices and trading volumes to spot patterns and predict future stock movements.

These key concepts of technical analysis help traders and investors understand and interpret market behavior to make informed decisions.

Moving Average: A moving average is a simple tool that helps you understand the overall direction of a stock's price over time by smoothing out the daily ups and downs. It's like calculating the average price of the stock over a certain number of days to see a clearer trend.

Think of a moving average like your grades in school. Instead of looking at just one test score, you average out your scores over the whole semester to see how well you're doing overall. If your grades have been going up, the average will show that you're improving.

Here are the key moving averages to look for:

The 50-day moving average (50 MA) shows the average stock price over the last 50 days. It's useful for spotting short- to mid-term trends. For example, if the current stock price is above the 50 MA, it generally means the stock is in an uptrend.

The 200-day moving average (200 MA) shows the average stock price over the last 200 days. It's important for identifying long-term trends. For example, if the current stock price is above the 200 MA, it usually means the stock is in a long-term uptrend.

When comparing the 200-day moving average, 50-day moving average, and the current stock price, you can gain insights into the stock's trend and potential market sentiment. Let's take a look at NVIDIA Corporation (NVDA) as a real-life example from July 2024:

- The 200-day moving average is $73.39
- The 50-day moving average is $109.16
- The current stock price is $129.62

Interpretation:

200-Day Moving Average ($73.39): The 200-day moving average is much lower than both the 50-day moving average and the current stock price. This indicates a strong long-term uptrend, as the stock price has been consistently moving upward over a significant period.

50-Day Moving Average ($109.16): The 50-day moving average is lower than the current stock price but higher than the 200-day moving average. This suggests a strong short- to medium-term uptrend. The stock has been performing well over the last few months.

Current Stock Price ($129.62): The current stock price is higher than both the 50-day and 200-day moving averages. This confirms the ongoing uptrend and indicates strong bullish sentiment among investors.

This means the stock is doing really well because its current price is higher than both the 50-day and 200-day moving averages. Investors are feeling positive about it, pushing the price up and showing confidence in the stock's future. The big difference between the current price and the moving averages shows the stock has been on a strong upward trend with significant recent gains. It's like the stock just had an energy drink and is sprinting ahead!

If you're thinking about investing, the current upward trend might offer a good buying opportunity, as long as you believe the stock will continue to perform well. However, be cautious of potential price corrections due to the significant gap between the current price and the moving averages, as stocks often pull back to their moving averages after rapid increases. Additionally, monitor the 50-day moving average ($109.16) and the 200-day moving average ($73.39) as potential support levels if the stock price starts to decline.

Price Patterns: Price patterns are visual formations on stock charts that help predict future price movements. There are two main types of price patterns: chart patterns and candlestick patterns. In this book, we will discuss chart patterns.

Chart Patterns like head and shoulders, double tops, and double bottoms, are shapes that form on the charts and signal potential changes in price direction. Candlestick Patterns are shapes made by individual price bars on a stock chart. These shapes help traders understand how the market feels and can show if prices might change direction. This helps traders decide when to buy or sell stocks.

Colors of Candlesticks:

- **Green Candlestick:** Indicates the stock price went up from where it opened, suggesting an upward trend.

- **Red Candlestick:** Indicates the stock price went down from where it opened, suggesting a downward trend.

Size of Candlesticks:

- **Large Candlesticks:** Show big price changes and strong market sentiment. A large green candlestick indicates strong buying and a positive outlook, while a large red candlestick indicates strong selling and a negative outlook.
- **Small Candlesticks:** Show little price change and can indicate indecision in the market.

By looking at these colors and sizes, traders can better predict price movements and make smarter trading decisions.

Chart and candlestick patterns are particularly popular among day traders and short-term traders because they help make quick trading decisions based on recent price movements. However, they can also be useful for swing traders, who hold positions for several days or weeks, and even long-term investors who want to refine their entry and exit points. Ideally, you want to buy your stock when it's at its lowest and sell it when it's at its highest.

Chapter 8

Risk Management: Balancing Risks Without Breaking a Sweat

So far, you've learned how to research and identify good companies, understand the numbers that indicate a healthy company, and analyze market trends and the economy. However, even with strong analysis, stocks can still fall. This is why it's essential to know when it's time to sell, whether temporarily or permanently.

Think of it like having home insurance. You've invested so much time and effort into building your beautiful life, turning your house into a home, and paying off the mortgage. Naturally, you want to protect your assets, which is why you insure your home. Similarly, some people choose where to live based on the risk of natural disasters. For example, flood zones are a no-go for many due to high risk. Others avoid tornado alley or hurricane zones. Maybe you were once comfortable living in a wildfire zone until it became a recurring threat, prompting you to move. It's perfectly okay and necessary to reevaluate your risk tolerance over time.

Ballet Flats or Stilettos? Assessing Your Financial Risk

Knowing your risk tolerance is crucial for making smart investment decisions. Risk tolerance refers to how much risk you can handle without feeling too stressed or uncomfortable. Here are some simple points to help you understand your risk tolerance and why it's important.

Personal Financial Situation: Think about how stable your income is. If you have a reliable income and a good emergency fund, you might be able to take on more investment risks. However, if you have a lot of debt or an unstable income, you might want to play it safer.

Investment Goals: Your goals can shape how much risk you should take. If

85

you're investing for something far in the future, you can afford to take more risks because you have time to recover from any losses. But if you need the money soon, you'll want to be more cautious. Think of it as planning a big vacation—if it's years away, you can save gradually, but if it's next month, you can't risk losing your deposit.

Emotional Comfort with Risk: Consider how you feel about losing money. Some people can handle market ups and downs without much worry, while others might get very stressed. Your past experiences with investments can also influence your risk tolerance. If you've ever freaked out over a bad haircut, you might want to avoid the rollercoaster of high-risk stocks!

Investment Knowledge and Experience: The more you know about investing and the markets, the more comfortable you might feel with taking risks. If you're just starting out, you might want to take it slow and learn as you go. Remember, you wouldn't dive into the deep end of the pool without learning to swim first!

Life Stage and Age: Younger investors often have a higher risk tolerance because they have more time to bounce back from losses. As you get older and closer to retirement, you might prefer safer investments. It's like choosing between a wild night out and a cozy night in—your preference might change over the years.

Understanding your risk tolerance involves looking at your financial situation, investment goals, emotional comfort with risk, knowledge, and life stage. By considering these factors, you can make informed decisions that suit your comfort level and financial objectives.

Investing can be a rewarding journey, but it's important to understand the potential bumps along the way. Just as gains can grow your wealth, losses can take a toll, and recovering from these losses requires significant growth. By understanding the percentage of growth needed to recover from various levels of losses, you can better gauge your risk tolerance and make more informed investment decisions.

Let's break down how much a stock would need to grow to recover from various losses:

- "Minor Bump": A 10% loss needs 11.11% growth to recover.
- "Speed Bump": A 20% loss needs 25% growth to recover.
- "Roadblock": A 30% loss needs 42.86% growth to recover.
- "Fender Bender": A 50% loss needs 100% growth to recover.
- "Major Crash": A 75% loss needs 300% growth to recover.
- "Total Wipeout": A 90% loss needs 900% growth to recover.
- "Off a Cliff": A 100% loss means there's no coming back.

This is why understanding and managing your risk tolerance is essential. Investing without managing risk is like walking a tightrope in stilettos!

Personally, I don't like letting my investments drop more than 25% to 30%. If a stock falls 50%, new investors often fall into the trap of thinking, "Well, I already lost this much..." Trust me, I've been there too in my early years. Unfortunately, those stocks never recovered, and I lost money. The company would have to grow 100% just to get back to its original price, which is not that easy or quick to achieve.

Take Kodak, for example. Kodak was once a giant in the photography industry, but as digital cameras became popular, Kodak's stock plummeted and never fully recovered. Despite still being in existence, the company has never regained its former value. So, it's better to be safe than sorry.

Divas and Downturns: Shielding Your Stocks with Stop-Loss Orders

Stop-loss orders are your safety net in the stock market, acting like a financial guardian angel to protect you from major losses. Imagine you've got a fabulous stock in your portfolio, but the market takes an unexpected nosedive. A stop-loss order automatically sells your stock when it hits a certain price, preventing you from losing more than you're comfortable with. Let's say you bought shares at $50 each, and they're now worth $60. You don't want to risk them dropping too far, so you decide that if the price falls to $55, you want to sell automatically. You can set this up easily through your online brokerage account. Just log in, find the stock you want to protect, enter the stop-loss price, and confirm the order. This way, you'll have peace of mind knowing you're automatically protected from significant losses, and you can focus on enjoying life instead of constantly monitoring your stocks. Think of stop-loss orders as your stylish financial seatbelt, keeping you secure as you navigate the twists and turns of the stock market.

High Heels and High Betas: Understanding Market Volatility

The **beta factor** is used to measure how much a stock's price moves compared to the overall market. The market, typically represented by a broad index like the S&P 500, has a beta of 1. If a stock has a beta greater than 1, it's more volatile than the market. For instance, if a stock has a beta of 1.5, it means the stock is 50% more volatile than the market, so it tends to move up and down more sharply. On the other hand, a beta less than 1 indicates that the stock is less volatile than the market. For example, a beta of 0.7 means the stock is 30% less volatile, moving more gently with market changes.

If the market's looking as unpredictable as a toddler's mood swings, it might be time to ditch those high-beta stocks faster than your last bad date. High-beta stocks can be risky when you expect the market to become unstable or go down because they tend to drop more than the market. Selling these stocks can help protect your investments from larger losses. On the other hand, if the market is expected to rise, keeping or even buying high-beta stocks can help you take advantage of their potential for higher gains.

Your own risk tolerance also plays a role. If you're becoming more cautious with your investments, perhaps because you're nearing retirement or have changed financial goals, you might decide to sell high-beta stocks and shift to more stable, low-beta stocks. This way, you can reduce the overall risk in your portfolio and feel more secure about your investments.

You can find a stock's beta on various financial websites like Yahoo Finance, Google Finance, or Market Watch in the detailed stock information or key statistics section.

Finding Your Market Capitalization Fit

Imagine you are a middleman for restaurants, buying shrimp from the market in the morning and delivering it to your regular restaurants afterward. These restaurants can only buy 20 pounds of shrimp each day because they don't have the capacity for more. Would you buy 100 pounds of shrimp, knowing you won't be able to sell the excess to the restaurant owners? Of course not.

Similarly, before we buy stocks, we should look at their market capitalization and trading volume. This helps us understand how easily we can sell the stocks if we need to.

Blue-Chip Stocks:
- Market Cap: Often over $100 billion.
- Characteristics: Large, well-established, and financially sound companies with a history of reliable earnings and dividends.
- Examples: Apple, Microsoft, Coca-Cola.
- Liquidity: High daily trading volumes, making them very liquid and easy to buy and sell without significantly affecting the stock price.
- Risk Management: Generally considered low-risk investments due to their stability and strong financials.

Large-Cap Stocks:
- Market Cap: Companies valued over $10 billion.
- Characteristics: Established companies with stable earnings and strong market positions.
- Examples: Alphabet (Google), Amazon, Johnson & Johnson.
- Liquidity: High daily trading volumes.
- Risk Management: Stable and less risky, similar to blue-chip stocks.

Mid-Cap Stocks:

- Market Cap: Companies valued between $2 billion and $10 billion.
- Characteristics: Companies that offer a balance between growth potential and stability.
- Examples: Netflix, Square.
- Liquidity: Moderate to high daily trading volumes.
- Risk Management: Balanced risk and growth potential.

Small-Cap Stocks:

- Market Cap: Companies valued under $2 billion.
- Characteristics: Smaller, often newer companies with higher growth potential but also higher risk.
- Examples: Etsy, Roku.
- Liquidity: Lower daily trading volumes, potentially harder to sell quickly.
- Risk Management: More volatile and risky, but with higher growth potential.

Micro-Cap Stocks:

- Market Cap: Companies valued between $50 million and $300 million.
- Characteristics: Very small, often new companies that may be in early growth stages.
- Examples: Chanticleer Holdings, Bridgeline Digital.
- Liquidity: Low daily trading volumes, can be difficult to buy and sell without affecting the price.
- Risk Management: Higher risk due to limited financial resources and greater volatility.

Nano-Cap Stocks:

- Market Cap: Companies valued under $50 million.
- Characteristics: Extremely small, highly speculative companies.
- Examples: OTC penny stocks, some very small biotech firms.
- Liquidity: Very low daily trading volumes, making it challenging to trade without significant price impact.
- Risk Management: Extremely high risk, often subject to high volatility and potential liquidity issues.

In summary, market capitalization is like the size tag on a dress – it helps investors figure out how big, risky, and valuable the company is. It's a go-to metric in investment analysis, index construction, and portfolio management.

Understanding market capitalization is crucial, but it's equally important to consider a stock's trading volume to assess its liquidity and market dynamics.

Lipstick and Liquidity: Understanding Trading Volume

Every company has its own trading volume, which refers to the number of shares traded (bought and sold) during a specific period, usually a single trading day. Trading volume is a vital metric because it provides insights into the liquidity and investor interest in a particular stock. Here's a breakdown of why trading volume matters and how it varies:

Liquidity:
- High Trading Volume: Indicates high liquidity, meaning shares can be bought and sold easily without significantly impacting the stock price. This is common in large-cap and blue-chip stocks like Apple (AAPL) or Microsoft (MSFT).
- Low Trading Volume: Indicates low liquidity, making it harder to buy or sell shares without affecting the stock price. This is typical for smaller companies, such as micro-cap and nano-cap stocks.

Price Stability:
- High Volume Stocks: Typically experience more stable price movements because there are many buyers and sellers. Sudden price changes are less likely.
- Low Volume Stocks: Can be more volatile and subject to larger price swings because there are fewer buyers and sellers, and large trades can impact the price significantly.

Investor Sentiment:
- Increasing Volume: Can indicate growing investor interest or concern, depending on whether the price is rising or falling. A surge in volume often accompanies major news or earnings reports.
- Decreasing Volume: May suggest waning interest in the stock, possibly leading to price stagnation or decline.

Market Signals:
- Volume Spikes: Large spikes in volume can signal potential reversals or continuations of trends. Traders often use volume data to confirm price movements and trends.

To summarize this, the trading volume is important because it helps us understand how easily a stock can be bought or sold (liquidity), how stable its price is, what investors think about it, and what might happen next in the market. When many shares are traded (high volume), it's easier to buy or sell the stock, and its price tends to be more stable. When fewer shares are traded (low volume), the stock can be more unpredictable and harder to trade. By keeping an eye on trading volume, investors can make smarter choices and better manage their investments.

When it comes to buying shares with the intention of being able to sell them quickly, a general guideline is to ensure that your trades do not significantly impact the stock's price. Here's a simple rule of thumb:

The 5% Rule: Aim to keep your trade size below 5% of the stock's average daily trading volume. For instance, if a stock has an average daily trading volume of 100,000 shares, you should avoid buying more than 5,000 shares at once.

When you keep your trade size small compared to the average daily trading volume, it's easier to buy or sell without changing the stock price much. If the trading volume is low and you try to sell a lot of shares, you might not find enough buyers. This can force you to hold onto the shares longer, possibly losing more value if the market is dropping. Large trades can make the stock price move a lot, especially in stocks that aren't traded much. By keeping your trades within 5% of the daily volume, you can avoid causing big price changes and potential losses.

How to Check Average Daily Trading Volume

- Financial Websites: Sites like Yahoo Finance, Google Finance, and MarketWatch display the average daily trading volume for stocks.
    - Example: Search for the stock by its ticker symbol and look for the "Volume" or "Average Volume" statistic.
- Brokerage Platforms: Most online brokerage accounts provide detailed stock information, including trading volume.

Mix and Match: Crafting a Diversified Portfolio

A stock portfolio is a collection of stocks, or shares of ownership in various companies, that an investor holds. It reflects the investor's overall strategy and is designed to meet their financial goals, whether it's generating income, achieving capital appreciation, or preserving wealth. Think of it as your chic handbag filled with stylish accessories! You're probably not walking around with 10 wallets in your purse. Instead, you might have a lip gloss, a wallet, sunglasses, and a deodorant. A portfolio is just like that—except instead of accessories, you've got shares of ownership in a variety of fabulous companies.

A well-rounded stock portfolio often includes a diverse mix of stocks from different industries, sectors, and sometimes even countries. This diversity helps spread risk because if one stock or sector doesn't perform well, another might do better and balance things out.

Not only does diversification help manage risk, but it can also boost your returns. Think of it as mixing trendy pieces with classic staples – you get the best of both worlds. This mix helps you capitalize on growth opportunities in various sectors and asset classes, ensuring you're ready for any financial runway.

Achieving your long-term financial goals is another big win of diversification. A diversified portfolio provides more consistent returns over time, like having a wardrobe that transitions smoothly from season to season. It makes your investments more resilient to market changes, ensuring you stay on track even when the financial weather gets stormy. This stability is key for growing your wealth steadily and reaching your financial milestones. And here's how you diversify your portfolio like you would mix your accessories in your purse to be ready for anything the day throws at you:

Spread Investments Across Sectors

Investing in different industries like technology, healthcare, finance, consumer goods, and energy is a smart way to avoid sector-specific risks. For example, let's say you've found 7 fabulous companies across 4 different sectors, and you have $10,000 to invest. You'd split that $10,000 into 4 equal parts, investing $2,500 in each sector. Just remember, aim to be invested in at least 3 different sectors to keep your portfolio stylishly diversified!

Now, why is it smart to invest in 3-5 different sectors? Imagine putting all your eggs in one basket—if that basket tips over, you're left with scrambled dreams. By spreading your investments across various sectors, you're diversifying your portfolio, which means you're not overly reliant on any single part of the economy. If one sector takes a nosedive, the others can help cushion the fall. Think of it as fashion insurance: if stripes go out of style, you've still got your trusty polka dots and floral prints to keep you looking fabulous! Investing in different sectors is like having a versatile wardrobe ready for any occasion, ensuring your financial style stays in vogue no matter what.

Spread Investments Across Beta Factors

We already determined that rebalancing your portfolio periodically is important. If high-beta stocks have performed well and now make up a larger portion of your investments than you intended, it might be time to sell some of these stocks to maintain a balanced and diversified portfolio. High-beta stocks can offer higher returns during market upswings but come with more risk. Low-beta stocks provide stability and can cushion your portfolio during downturns.

Remember, the market has a beta of 1. A stock with a beta higher than 1 is more volatile (risky) than the market, and a stock with a beta lower than 1 is less volatile.

Mix Different Types of Stocks

While this book mainly prioritizes finding growth stocks from top-notch companies with strong fundamentals, competitive advantages, and capable management, it's important to know about other types of stocks that investors use for diversification: value stocks and dividend stocks. Especially dividend stocks might be a good option for you once you reach the financial freedom stage discussed at the beginning of the book and want to shift to more stable growth with regular income. Here's how you can spot them.

Growth Stocks: Growth stocks are shares of companies expected to grow faster than average compared to other companies. These companies usually reinvest their earnings into the business to help it grow, rather than paying out dividends to shareholders.

Characteristics:

- High potential for significant increase in value.
- Often found in industries like technology or biotech that are expanding rapidly.
- Typically have high price-to-earnings (P/E) ratios because investors expect strong future growth.

How to Spot Them:

- Look for companies with strong revenue and earnings growth.
- Check if the company is in a high-growth industry.
- Review the company's P/E ratio; growth stocks usually have higher P/E ratios.
- Examples: Tesla (TSLA), Amazon (AMZN).

Value Stocks: Value stocks are shares of companies that are considered undervalued compared to their true worth. These companies are often mature and stable, but their stock prices might be lower due to short-term issues.

Characteristics:

- Typically have lower P/E ratios.
- Often pay dividends.
- May be temporarily out of favor with the market.

How to Spot Them:

- Look for companies with low P/E ratios compared to others in the same industry.
- Check for high dividend yields, which show that the company returns profits to shareholders.
- Review financial metrics like price-to-book (P/B) ratio and price-to-sales (P/S) ratio.
- Examples: Johnson & Johnson (JNJ), Coca-Cola (KO).

Dividend Stocks: Dividend stocks are shares of companies that regularly pay out part of their earnings to shareholders as dividends. These stocks are popular with investors who want regular income.

Characteristics:
- Provide regular income through dividends.
- Typically found in stable industries like utilities, consumer goods, and finance.
- Companies usually have a history of stable and increasing dividends.

How to Spot Them:
- Look for companies with a consistent history of paying dividends.
- Check the dividend yield, which is the annual dividend payment divided by the stock price.
- Review the company's dividend payout ratio to ensure the dividend is sustainable.
- Examples: Procter & Gamble (PG), Exxon Mobil Corporation (XOM), Bayerische Motoren Werke AG (BMW)

Keep It Classy

"If you're emotional about investing, you're not going to do well" – Waffen Buffet

Imagine you've just gone through a shocking breakup. The last thing you want to do is become the psycho ex-girlfriend that men always seem to have been in a relationship with. We will take the high road and show that we're so much better off without him, anyway. Of course, at first, you're devastated. The initial shock feels like the market plummeting overnight. You might spend a couple of days in your pajamas, binge-watching sad movies, and eating ice cream. But then, you remember who you are and decide it's time to bounce back.

You book a spa day to pamper yourself. You get a massage, a facial, and your nails done. It's all about self-care and regaining your confidence. This is like educating yourself about market cycles and creating a solid investment plan. You're preparing yourself to handle the situation with grace.

Next, you decide to diversify your activities. You reconnect with friends, pick up a new hobby, or dive into a good book. Diversification in your social life ensures you're not putting all your emotional eggs in one basket, just like spreading your investments across different asset classes.

Then comes the big day: you put on your best outfit, do your hair and makeup, and step out looking better than ever. You're not hiding from the world; you're showing up stronger. This is the equivalent of sticking to your investment plan, staying the course, and maintaining perspective. You know that short-term pain can lead to long-term gains.

Throughout this journey, you practice mindfulness. Maybe you take up meditation or yoga, focusing on what you can control and letting go of what you can't. This helps you stay grounded and calm, just like handling market volatility without reacting emotionally to every fluctuation.

In the end, you emerge from the breakup not just as your old self, but as a more resilient and confident version. You've found your inner calm and learned to navigate the ups and downs with grace. The same approach can help you handle the chaos of market volatility, allowing you to achieve your financial goals with discipline and patience.

You may need to stock up on your knowledge. Understand that markets go through cycles of ups and downs. Volatility is a natural part of investing, just like relationships have their highs and lows. Look at historical data to see how markets have rebounded from past downturns. This can provide reassurance during turbulent times.

Focus on your long-term goals and remember that short-term market ups and downs often don't affect your long-term success. Steer clear of overreacting, as making decisions based on emotions can result in purchasing at high prices and selling at low ones. Stay calm, make choices based on logic and strategy, and learn from your mistakes to become wiser and more resilient. Practice patience and discipline by staying committed to your strategy, resisting the urge to frequently check or alter your investments based on short-term movements. Trust that your long-term plan will yield results over time.

Now that you know how to spot growth stocks and invest wisely, don't get swayed by traders shouting "buy" or "sell." You don't know what kind of trader they are – a day trader's strategy is very different from a long-term investor's. Stick to your plan and focus on what works for you, and you'll be more likely to achieve financial freedom. And always remember: While the stock market is beyond your control, how you respond to it is entirely up to you!

PART III

Making Money Moves

Chapter 9

Picking Your Brokerage BFF

You've probably heard the term stockbrokers somewhere before, but what really is a stockbroker?

Stockbrokers are the fabulous middlemen in the financial world, making it a breeze for you to buy and sell stocks, bonds, and mutual funds. Whether they work alone or for a big company, brokers play a crucial role in ensuring the smooth operation of financial markets. You can find brokers at major banks and financial institutions, many of which offer comprehensive brokerage services. And let's not forget the online brokers – just a quick web search away! Organizations like the Financial Industry Regulatory Authority (FINRA) provide directories of licensed brokers, and you can always ask for recommendations from your well-connected friends, family, or financial advisors.

Choosing the right broker is like finding the perfect shopping buddy – it all depends on what you need and want. It's a good idea to do some research and compare different brokers to find one that offers the services, tools, and support you need. And just like asking a fashion-savvy friend for advice, talking to a financial advisor can give you helpful insights.

There are various types of brokers available, each with distinct characteristics:

Full-service brokers: Full-service brokers are real people who provide personalized investment advice, financial planning, and portfolio management services. They often have titles like financial advisor, investment advisor, or wealth manager, making them your personal financial guides. These brokers offer customized advice and hands-on management of your investments, ensuring you have a dedicated advisor or even a whole team to help you out.

In terms of services, full-service brokers provide everything from investment

96

advice and research to retirement planning, tax advice, and portfolio management. Some big names in this category include Merrill Lynch, Morgan Stanley, and UBS. They're like a one-stop shop for all your financial needs.

However, this level of service comes at a cost. Full-service brokers typically charge higher commissions per trade, usually ranging from $50 to $200. They may also impose an annual fee based on a percentage of your assets under management, which is usually between 1% to 2%. Additionally, they can charge hourly fees for financial planning and consultations, ranging from $100 to $400 per hour.

So, if you're looking for a personalized touch and a wide array of services, full-service brokers might be the way to go. Just be prepared to pay a bit more for that hands-on assistance!

Despite that, it's important to stay vigilant and informed about your investments. Always remember that no one cares about your money more than you do! Full-service brokers make their money through commissions, fees, and account management charges. They may also receive compensation through sales loads on mutual funds, markups on bond prices, and other financial products. This essentially means that you still need to know what you're doing. The brokers do not bear the risk – it is still your money on the line. When your investments perform poorly, they continue to get paid by other customers, while you might be left with nothing if you don't do your own research.

Discount brokers, also known as automated brokers, provide platforms for self-directed investors to trade and manage their own investments with minimal human intervention. Some even offer robo-advisory services that use algorithms to manage portfolios based on the client's risk profile and investment goals. These brokers typically operate through automated online platforms, making it convenient for investors to handle their trades and account management independently. Additionally, some discount brokers offer access to financial advisors or consultants, either for an additional fee or as part of premium services. While customer support representatives are available to assist, most of the process is managed online, ensuring a streamlined and efficient experience for investors.

Compared to full-service brokers, discount brokers offer fewer services but at a much lower cost. Their primary focus is on executing trades and providing basic research tools. Some well-known examples of discount brokers include Charles Schwab, Fidelity, and TD Ameritrade. These brokers are perfect for investors who prefer a DIY approach to managing their portfolios.

In terms of costs, discount brokers charge lower commissions, often between $5 to $25 per trade, though many have now moved to zero-commission trading for stocks and ETFs. Account fees are also lower or sometimes nonexistent, although some brokers might charge inactivity fees or fees for additional services. This makes discount brokers a cost-effective choice for those who are comfortable managing their investments online with fewer frills.

Online brokers provide trading platforms that allow investors to trade stocks online with minimal human interaction. These brokers typically have lower fees and commissions, making them a cost-effective option for many investors. An example of a well-known online broker is Robinhood. This platform is designed for the modern investor who prefers to manage their trades and investments online with an easy swipe up or down. Unlike full-service and discount brokers, which often offer tax-advantaged accounts, some online brokers primarily offer simple trading accounts, which might be less attractive if you want to minimize taxes.

Many online brokers offer zero-commission trading for stocks and ETFs, making them highly attractive to cost-conscious investors. However, they may charge fees for options trading, typically around $0.50 to $1.00 per contract, as well as margin interest and fees for premium services. Account fees are usually minimal but can include small charges for wire transfers, paper statements, or other account-related services.

Overall, online brokers are a great choice if you're looking for a low-cost way to trade stocks and don't need a lot of hand-holding. With a range of tools and resources available, you can take control of your investments and manage them from the comfort of your own home.

To make the most of your online trading experience, it's important to have a clear understanding of the fees and commissions charged by your brokerage account. These charges can dramatically impact your investment returns over time. By minimizing these costs, you get to keep more of your hard-earned money. Knowing the fees and commissions also helps you compare different brokers and choose the one that offers the best value for your investment style. Plus, being aware of all potential fees ensures there are no surprises – because nobody likes unexpected charges, especially when they're attacking your wallet!

To minimize fees, you can choose commission-free options by looking for brokers that offer commission-free trading. Maintaining the required minimum balance can help you avoid pesky account maintenance fees. Monitoring your activity levels to avoid fees and choosing a broker that doesn't charge for inactivity can also help.

While it's important to grasp the fees involved, it's equally vital to know the capabilities of your broker. Just because they're stockbrokers does not mean they can trade on every stock exchange. Every stockbroker needs to meet specific criteria to ensure they can handle transactions on multiple stock exchanges. This ability can significantly impact your investment strategy, particularly if you aim to diversify your portfolio internationally.

Having access to multiple stock exchanges allows you to diversify your investments more effectively. Diversification reduces risk by spreading your investments across different markets and asset classes. For instance, if your broker can trade on international exchanges, you can invest in foreign companies, providing growth opportunities not available in domestic markets

Let's take a look at some of the major international stock exchanges:

New York Stock Exchange (NYSE): Is the largest stock exchange in the world by market capitalization and located in the United States. It lists many of the largest companies globally.

NASDAQ: The NASDAQ is known for its high concentration of technology and growth-oriented companies. It is the second-largest exchange in the world by market capitalization and also residing within the United States.

Shanghai Stock Exchange (SSE): Located in China, the SSE is one of the largest stock exchanges globally by market capitalization. It plays a significant role in the Chinese economy.

Hong Kong Stock Exchange (HKEX): Based in Hong Kong, HKEX is one of the largest exchanges in Asia and the world, listing many leading companies from Hong Kong, China, and other parts of Asia.

Euronext: A pan-European stock exchange operating in multiple countries, including France, the Netherlands, Belgium, Portugal, and Ireland. Euronext is one of the largest stock exchanges in Europe by market capitalization.

Tokyo Stock Exchange (TSE): The largest stock exchange in Japan and one of the biggest in Asia. The TSE lists many of Japan's major corporations.

Shenzhen Stock Exchange (SZSE): Another significant exchange in China, the SZSE is known for its listings of high-tech and growth enterprises, making it one of the largest by market capitalization.

London Stock Exchange (LSE): Based in the United Kingdom, the LSE is one of the oldest and most prominent stock exchanges globally, listing a wide range of international companies.

Toronto Stock Exchange (TSX): Located in Canada, the TSX is one of the largest stock exchanges in North America, known for its significant listings in the mining and energy sectors.

National Stock Exchange of India (NSE): Located in Mumbai, the NSE is one of India's leading stock exchanges, known for its advanced electronic trading system and large market capitalization.

Investing in multiple stock exchanges lets you explore global markets, giving you the chance to grow your investments by tapping into emerging markets and benefiting from economic trends in different regions. This can really boost your portfolio by looking beyond your home country.

In today's fast-moving global economy, having a broker that can trade on multiple exchanges gives you an edge. You can quickly react to global market trends and news, making smart investment decisions that take advantage of opportunities around the world. Having a broker who trades internationally is like having a multilingual guide for your money – it navigates through different markets with ease.

Protecting Your Investments:

When it comes to investing, knowing how much of your money is insured is absolutely crucial. Why? Because if your brokerage or bank goes bankrupt, you want to make sure your hard-earned money is safe. Start by checking their insurance package to see how much of your funds are covered—it can give you much-needed peace of mind.

For instance, the Securities Investor Protection Corporation (SIPC) typically covers up to $500,000 in securities, with a $250,000 limit for cash. Knowing this helps you plan better. On the other hand, the Federal Deposit Insurance Corporation (FDIC) provides deposit insurance to account holders in U.S. commercial banks and savings institutions. This insurance guarantees the safety of an individual's accounts up to $250,000 per person, per insured bank, for each account ownership category. It covers all types of deposits, including savings accounts, checking accounts, and certificates of deposit (CDs).

By understanding these protections, you can ensure your investments and savings are secure, allowing you to invest with confidence and ease.

When choosing a broker, always make sure they are insured by the SIPC and FDIC. If they don't offer this insurance, it's a good idea to find a different broker. Additionally, many brokerage firms purchase extra insurance, often referred to as "excess SIPC" or "supplemental insurance," to provide additional protection beyond SIPC limits. This coverage, provided through private insurers, typically offers higher limits on both cash and securities. The specifics of this extra coverage can vary significantly between brokerages.

For instance, a brokerage might offer additional insurance that covers each customer up to several million dollars, with separate limits for cash and securities. It's crucial to check with your specific brokerage to understand the details of any additional insurance they offer, including coverage limits and the conditions under which the insurance applies.

If you're approaching the insurance limit, it's smart to diversify and spread your investments across multiple brokerage firms. This way, you ensure that more of your money is protected. Imagine the relief of knowing your investments are safe no matter what happens! Plus, diversifying can also lead to exploring new investment opportunities. Always make sure your financial safety net is strong – it's one of the best ways to secure your financial future. So, take a moment to check those insurance details and protect your investments wisely!

Chapter 10

Nurturing Your Investments

Imagine your portfolio to be like a garden full of houseplants. Both require care, attention, and a bit of strategy to thrive. Just as you wouldn't water your plants every day, you don't need to obsess over your stocks daily either. In this chapter, we'll explore how a little regular maintenance can go a long way in keeping both your houseplants and your investments healthy and flourishing.

Spend about 30 minutes a week checking on your stocks. Don't overwhelm yourself by managing more than 5-10 stocks at a time. This amount is manageable and helps you stay on top of things without stress. Set a weekly reminder for this dedicated time. Just like with houseplants, stick to an amount you can handle. More houseplants mean more work, and the same goes for stocks. Keeping track of 5 to 10 good companies is plenty.

If you occasionally forget to check, it's not the end of the world. However, neglecting your stocks for long periods can be harmful, just like forgetting to water your plants. Remember that consistency doesn't ensure success, but a lack of consistency ensures failure. During your 30-minute weekly check-in, keep up with company news and monitor the stock market's progress.

Once a year, just like repotting your houseplants, it's time for a big financial review. Conduct a thorough analysis of each company you own shares in. Check all their financials and track their progress. Are they still growing? While companies release quarterly statements, it's more important to look at their annual performance.

Just like seasonal plants, some companies, like those selling Christmas decor, will have different numbers in off-quarters compared to their peak season. By focusing on the annual performance, you get a clearer picture of their overall trajectory and can make informed decisions about whether to continue holding or adjust your portfolio. This annual review ensures that your investments are still aligned with your financial goals and helps you stay proactive in managing your portfolio.

Imagine this like providing your plants with new soil and more room to grow. Examine key indicators such as revenue growth, profit margins, and debt levels. Consider the company's market position and competitive landscape. Are they innovating and expanding? Are they maintaining a strong customer base? This comprehensive review helps you understand the long-term health and potential of your investments.

Much like caring for your houseplants requires regular attention and occasional replanting, managing your investments involves periodic rebalancing to keep them healthy and growing. Analyzing and adjusting your portfolio once a year is essential for keeping your preferred risk level intact and ensuring that your investments remain aligned with your financial goals. Over time, some of your investments may perform better than others, leading your portfolio to deviate from its original diversified spread.

An annual review is necessary for evenly distributing your stocks, just as we discussed in our previous chapter on diversification to spread risk across different sectors, beta factor, and stock types. This review is also a good time to let go of underperforming stocks. For example, if a stock is moving into its maturity phase with less growth potential but stable dividends, and you prefer more growth prospects to meet your financial goals, it might be time to sell. Similarly, if a stock is entering its decline phase, you should consider selling it quickly. By now, you should be able to identify these signs by examining financial reports and act accordingly.

Chapter 11

Tax Time Tactics

Taxes might not be the most glamorous part of investing, but understanding how to navigate them can save you a significant amount of money. Think of it as mastering the art of dodging the Tax Man, so it doesn't feel like you're donating your hard-earned cash to a black hole. In this chapter, we'll explore various accounts and tactics to avoid or defer taxes, turning you into a financial ninja who slices through tax liabilities with style.

We'll cover everything from capital gains tax and tax-advantaged accounts to clever strategies like tax-loss harvesting and using qualified dividends. By the end of this chapter, you'll have a toolkit of tax-efficient techniques that'll make you feel like a pro, keeping more of your money working for you. So, let's dive in and learn how to be smart about our taxes and see our investments grow!

Capital gains are the profits you make from selling an asset, like stocks, bonds, real estate, or other investments. Managing these gains involves various strategies to reduce the amount of tax you owe. Think of capital gains management as the ultimate game of dodgeball, where the goal is to dodge as many tax hits as possible.

Why is this so important? Proper management of capital gains can significantly reduce your tax burden, allowing you to keep more of your investment earnings. By utilizing legal strategies, you can defer or minimize taxes, ultimately boosting your overall returns and helping you achieve your financial goals more efficiently. This is crucial for any taxable investment account in the USA, including individual brokerage accounts, joint accounts, and trust accounts where capital gains taxes apply.

Now, let's talk about the grandmaster of this game: Warren Buffett. Buffett is a pro at minimizing capital gains tax by holding onto investments with long-term potential. By not frequently buying and selling stocks, he avoids the capital gains taxes associated with short-term trading. Taxes on unrealized gains (the increase in value of investments that have not been sold) are not due until the asset is sold. This deferral allows his investments to compound over time, increasing his wealth more efficiently. Plus, dividends provide a steady stream of income without the need to sell shares, thus avoiding capital gains taxes.

Berkshire Hathaway, Buffett's investment vehicle, benefits from tax-efficient structures. As a corporation, Berkshire can reinvest its earnings without distributing them as dividends, thus avoiding the double taxation that individual investors might face (corporate tax on earnings and personal income tax on dividends). This approach contrasts sharply with other investors who constantly buy and sell, paying a lot more in taxes as a result.

Here are some strategies to minimize or defer capital gains taxes on stock investments:

Hold Investments Longer

Holding investments for the long term is a smart tax strategy because long-term capital gains (from assets held for more than one year) are taxed at a lower rate than short-term gains. Here's why this matters:

When you sell an asset that you've held for less than a year, any profit you make is considered a short-term capital gain and is taxed at your ordinary income tax rate, which can be quite high depending on your income level. However, if you hold onto that asset for more than a year before selling, the profit is considered a long-term capital gain and is taxed at a significantly lower rate.

In the U.S., long-term capital gains tax rates are generally 0%, 15%, or 20%, depending on your income level, which is often much lower than the rates for ordinary income.

By holding investments for over a year, you can take advantage of these lower tax rates, resulting in substantial tax savings. This strategy not only helps you keep more of your investment returns but also encourages a long-term investment mindset, which can be beneficial for growing your wealth over time.

Additionally, holding your investments for the long term allows them to compound, which can significantly increase their value. As we discussed in previous chapters, compounding is the process where the earnings on your investments generate their own earnings. Over time, this compounding effect can lead to exponential growth in the value of your investments, making them much more valuable than if you were to cash out early.

So, think of holding investments longer as not just a tax-saving strategy but also a way to let your investments mature and grow. Just let your investments do their thing and enjoy the lower tax bill when you finally cash in! It's a win-win: lower taxes and a growing investment portfolio!

Tax-Loss Harvesting

Tax-loss harvesting is a strategy used to reduce your taxable capital gains by selling investments that are currently at a loss.

Here's how it works: Imagine you have a variety of investments in your portfolio. Some have increased in value, while others have decreased. When you sell an investment that has increased in value, you realize a capital gain, which is subject to taxes. However, if you also sell an investment that has decreased in value, you realize a capital loss. By selling the investment at a loss, you can offset the gains from your other investments.

For example, if you made $10,000 in capital gains from selling some stocks but also realized $4,000 in losses from selling other stocks that went below your comfort zone, your taxable capital gains would be reduced to $6,000 ($10,000 gains - $4,000 losses).

This strategy helps lower your overall tax bill because you're using the losses to cancel out some of the gains. It's like getting a discount on your taxes for making smart investment moves. Tax-loss harvesting can be especially advantageous at year-end when aiming to minimize your tax burden.

Keep the "wash sale" rule in mind, which prohibits repurchasing a substantially identical security within 30 days before or after selling it at a loss. If you violate this rule, the loss will be disallowed for tax purposes. In essence, tax-loss harvesting allows you to make the most of a down market by turning losses into tax-saving opportunities, helping you keep more of your investment earnings. So, think of it as a financial silver lining — turning your lemons into lemonade, or in this case, your losses into tax savings!

Utilize Tax-Advantaged Accounts

Tax-advantaged accounts are financial accounts that offer special tax benefits, making them powerful tools for building wealth and minimizing tax liabilities. These accounts include retirement accounts, health savings accounts, and education savings accounts. They provide various tax benefits, such as tax-deferred growth, tax-free withdrawals, or tax deductions on contributions.

The primary reason to use tax-advantaged accounts is to minimize your tax burden and maximize your investment growth. These accounts allow your investments to grow either tax-deferred or tax-free, which can significantly enhance your overall returns. Additionally, some accounts offer tax deductions on contributions, reducing your taxable income in the year you contribute.

Types of Tax-Advantaged Accounts

Retirement Accounts

- **Traditional IRA:** This account allows you to contribute pre-tax dollars, meaning you may be able to deduct your contributions from your taxable income for the year. This can lower your current tax bill and potentially place you in a lower tax bracket. The investments within the account grow tax-deferred, meaning you won't pay taxes on the earnings until you withdraw the money in retirement.

  When you withdraw funds from a Traditional IRA in retirement, these withdrawals are taxed as ordinary income. This means you will pay income tax on the amount you withdraw based on your tax bracket at the time of withdrawal. Generally, withdrawals are penalty-free after you reach the age of 59½. However, if you withdraw funds before this age, you may incur a 10% early withdrawal penalty in addition to the income tax. Traditional IRAs also have required minimum distributions (RMDs), which means you must start taking withdrawals from your account by April 1st of the year following the year you turn 73 (as of 2023). The amount of the RMD is based on your life expectancy and account balance, and failing to take the required distribution can result in substantial penalties.

- **Roth IRA:** Contributions are made with after-tax dollars, allowing your investments to grow tax-free. This means that, while you won't get a tax deduction for your contributions now, all future earnings and qualified withdrawals in retirement are completely tax-free. To qualify for tax-free withdrawals, the account must be at least five years old, and you must be at least 59½ years old or meet other specific criteria, such as using the funds for a first-time home purchase.

  The benefit of a Roth IRA is that you pay taxes on the money you contribute now. Upon retirement, you can withdraw your contributions and earnings tax-free, providing a substantial financial benefit in the future. Additionally, unlike traditional IRAs, Roth IRAs do not have required minimum distributions (RMDs) during the account holder's lifetime, allowing your savings to continue growing tax-free for as long as you like.

  By contributing to a Roth IRA, you can enjoy the peace of mind knowing that your future withdrawals will not be subject to taxes, giving you greater financial flexibility and security in retirement.

- **401(k):** A 401(k) is an employer-sponsored retirement plan where your contributions are often tax-deductible, and your investments grow tax-deferred, meaning you won't pay taxes on your contributions or earnings until you withdraw the money in retirement. Some employers also offer a Roth 401(k) option, which allows for tax-free withdrawals in retirement. Take full advantage of employer-sponsored 401(k) plans, especially if your employer offers matching contributions – it's essentially free money added to your retirement savings. Consider SEP IRAs or Solo 401(k) plans if you are self-employed. These offer greater contribution caps and comparable tax advantages. You can reduce your taxable income now by contributing to these accounts, potentially placing you in a lower tax bracket and lowering your current tax bill. However, you will pay taxes on the withdrawals later, when you cash out in retirement. Maximize your contributions to these plans to enjoy tax benefits now and build a solid foundation for your future! Equivalent retirement savings plans for other professions include the 403(b) Plan for teachers, the 457(b) Plan for first responders, and the Thrift Savings Plan (TSP) for military members.

Health Savings Accounts (HSAs)

A Health Savings Account (HSA) is a tax-advantaged account designed to help individuals with high-deductible health plans (HDHPs) save for medical expenses. HSAs offer a unique triple tax advantage, making them a powerful tool for managing healthcare costs and even retirement savings. Contributions to an HSA are made with pre-tax dollars, which means they can be deducted from your taxable income, lowering your current tax bill. Some employers also contribute to employees' HSAs, adding to the savings.

The money in an HSA grows tax-free. You can invest the funds in various investment options, such as mutual funds or stocks, allowing your savings to grow over time. The interest and investment earnings in the account are not affected by federal income tax. This makes it easier for your balance to grow faster.

Withdrawals from an HSA are tax-free when used for qualified medical expenses. These expenses include a wide range of healthcare costs, such as doctor visits, prescription medications, dental care, and even some over-the-counter drugs. If you withdraw funds for non-medical expenses before the age of 65, you will owe income tax on the amount and a 20% penalty. However, after age 65, you can withdraw funds for any purpose without the penalty, although non-medical withdrawals will still be subject to income tax.

Health Savings Accounts (HSAs) offer several compelling benefits. They provide a triple tax advantage: Contributions are tax-deductible, earnings grow tax-free, and withdrawals for qualified medical expenses are also tax-free. Unlike Flexible Spending Accounts (FSAs), HSAs are not "use-it-or-lose-it" – the funds roll over year to year, allowing your savings to accumulate over time. Additionally, HSAs are portable, meaning they remain with you even if you change jobs or retire. Beyond immediate healthcare costs, HSAs can also serve as an additional retirement savings vehicle.

Education Savings Accounts:

- **529 Plans:** 529 Plans provide a tax-advantaged way to save for education expenses. Contributions are made with after-tax dollars but grow tax-free, and withdrawals for qualified education expenses are tax-free. These plans offer significant benefits, including state tax deductions or credits, high contribution limits, and flexibility in changing beneficiaries. By utilizing a 529 Plan, you can effectively save for future education costs and take advantage of the significant tax benefits they offer.

- **Coverdell Education Savings Accounts (ESAs):** Coverdell Education Savings Accounts (ESAs) provide a tax-advantaged way to save for a wide range of education expenses, from kindergarten through college. Contributions are made with after-tax dollars but grow tax-free, and withdrawals for qualified education expenses are tax-free. These accounts offer significant benefits, including flexibility in covering K-12 expenses, a broad selection of investment options, and the ability to grow funds tax-free. By utilizing a Coverdell ESA, families can effectively save for their children's education and take advantage of the associated tax benefits. Using tax-advantaged accounts is like having a secret weapon in your financial toolkit. These accounts help you grow your wealth while keeping the tax man at bay. Whether you're saving for retirement, healthcare, or your kids' education, these accounts offer amazing tax benefits that make your money work harder for you.

Gifting Appreciated Assets

Appreciated assets are investments that have increased in value since you acquired them. For example, if you bought stock for $1,000 and it's now worth $5,000, you have an appreciated asset with a gain of $4,000. Gifting appreciated assets, like stocks, can be a savvy move both for you and the recipient. Here's how it works and why it can be beneficial:

Transferring the Stock: Instead of selling the stock and then gifting the proceeds, you transfer the ownership of the stock directly to the recipient. This way, you avoid realizing a capital gain and the associated taxes.

Recipient's Cost Basis: The recipient inherits your original cost basis and holding period. Using the example above, if you bought the stock for $1,000 and it's now worth $5,000, the recipient's cost basis is $1,000. If they sell the stock immediately, they will realize the $4,000 gain and pay the capital gains tax based on their tax rate.

Avoiding Immediate Tax Impact: By gifting the appreciated stock, you avoid paying the capital gains tax. This can be particularly beneficial if you're in a high tax bracket and the recipient is in a lower tax bracket. The recipient may end up paying less in taxes when they eventually sell the stock.

Gifting appreciated stocks offers several benefits. First, it provides tax efficiency by allowing you to avoid paying capital gains tax on the appreciated value of the stock, while the recipient may benefit from a lower tax rate. Second, if you donate appreciated stock to a qualified charity, you can avoid capital gains tax altogether and potentially receive a charitable deduction for the full market value of the stock. Finally, gifting appreciated assets can help reduce the size of your taxable estate, which can be advantageous for estate planning purposes.

Let's say you want to help a family member with college expenses. Instead of giving them cash, you gift them appreciated stock. You bought the stock for $2,000, and it's now worth $10,000. By transferring the stock to them, you avoid paying capital gains tax on the $8,000 gain. If the family member is in a lower tax bracket, they will pay less in capital gains taxes when they sell the stock. Plus, if they need the funds for qualified education expenses, there might be additional tax benefits or opportunities to offset gains with education credits.

Gifting appreciated assets like stocks can be a strategic way to manage your tax liability while benefiting the recipient. By transferring the stock directly, you avoid realizing a capital gain and the associated taxes, potentially lowering the overall tax burden if the recipient is in a lower tax bracket. This strategy can also be a valuable tool in charitable giving and estate planning.

Dividend Income Strategies

When you have stocks that also pay a dividend, you can employ several strategies to maximize your returns and manage your taxes efficiently. Here are two key strategies to think about:

Qualified Dividends: Choosing stocks that offer qualified dividends can be a smart investment approach. Qualified dividends are dividends paid by U.S. corporations (and some foreign corporations) that meet specific IRS criteria. The big advantage here is that these dividends are taxed at the lower long-term capital gains rates instead of the higher ordinary income tax rates. This can significantly reduce your tax bill. To benefit from the lower tax rates on qualified dividends:

- Invest in Eligible Stocks: Ensure the stocks you invest in pay qualified dividends. Typically, most blue-chip companies and other established firms with a history of paying dividends meet these criteria.
- Holding Period Requirements: To ensure the dividends are qualified, you need to own the stock for over 60 days within the 121-day period that starts 60 days before the ex-dividend date. This encourages a longer-term investment strategy, which can also help with overall portfolio stability.

Dividend Reinvestment Plans (DRIPs): Another effective strategy is to enroll in Dividend Reinvestment Plans (DRIPs). DRIPs allow you to automatically reinvest your dividends to purchase more shares of the company's stock instead of receiving cash payouts. This can be a powerful way to grow your investment over time through the magic of compounding. Advantages of DRIPs include:

- Compounding Growth: By reinvesting your dividends, you buy more shares, which in turn can earn more dividends, creating a snowball effect of compounding growth.
- Tax Deferral: While you still owe taxes on dividends in the year they are paid, reinvesting them can help defer selling decisions and the associated capital gains taxes. However, it's important to keep track of your reinvested dividends, as they will affect your cost basis when you eventually sell the shares.
- No Commissions: Many DRIPs allow you to reinvest dividends without paying brokerage commissions, making it a cost-effective way to grow your holdings.

When you have stocks that also pay a dividend, leveraging strategies like investing in qualified dividend-paying stocks and enrolling in DRIPs can significantly enhance your investment returns while offering tax benefits. Qualified dividends are taxed at lower rates, reducing your overall tax burden, while DRIPs allow for compounding growth and potential tax deferral. By incorporating these strategies into your investment plan, you can maximize your dividend income and build a more robust portfolio over time. So, start thinking of those dividend-paying stocks not just as income sources, but as powerful tools for long-term growth and tax efficiency!

How to Minimize Capital Gains Tax When Rebalancing Your Portfolio
Let's address rebalancing your portfolio and taxes. Since rebalancing is essential to maintain a desired level of risk and to ensure that your investments stay aligned with your financial goals. However, it can trigger capital gains taxes if you're not careful. Here are two savvy strategies to minimize those taxes while keeping your portfolio in tip-top shape:

Gradual Rebalancing: Instead of a complete overhaul, rebalance your portfolio gradually. By selling a little at a time, you spread out your tax obligations and avoid a hefty bill all at once. Think of it like slowly reducing sugar in your diet rather than quitting cold turkey. This approach not only helps manage your tax impact but also allows you to stay flexible and adjust your strategy as market conditions change.

Suppose you need to reduce your holdings in a stock that has appreciated significantly. By selling a portion each year, you can potentially keep your total income (including capital gains) within a lower tax bracket. For instance, long-term capital gains are taxed at 0%, 15%, or 20% depending on your total taxable income. Spreading out the sales might help you stay in the 15% bracket rather than jumping into the 20% bracket.

Consider the Tax Impact: Always calculate if the benefits of rebalancing outweigh the tax costs. Sometimes paying a little capital gains tax is worth the peace of mind that comes with a well-balanced, diversified portfolio. It's like splurging on that designer piece you've been eyeing—it's an investment in your overall style and confidence!

If your portfolio has drifted significantly from your target allocation, and the imbalance poses a risk, the cost of paying some capital gains tax might be a small price for reducing that risk. Run the numbers to determine the best course of action.

In summary, smart tax strategies can make a huge difference in boosting your investment returns. By using tactics like gradual rebalancing, tax-loss harvesting, and playing the qualified dividends game, you can keep more of your hard-earned money where it belongs – in your fabulous portfolio. Remember, the key is to stay proactive and savvy about taxes. With these tax time tactics, you're not just an investor; you're a financial diva, slashing tax liabilities with style and grace!

Chapter 12

Keep Growing, Keep Glowing

Making money is one thing; keeping it is another. Earning money requires taking risks, staying optimistic, and putting yourself out there. Holding onto that money, however, demands humility, frugality, and a constant dedication to learning and adapting. Here's how to stay on top of your financial game and keep that glow going strong:

Getting to know the companies you invest in should be a top priority. After all, you wouldn't just hand a stranger $1,000 and hope they double it, would you? The same logic applies to investing. Dive into the company's financial health, business model, and leadership. This is why we focus on a maximum of 10 companies; the fewer you have, the better you can get to know them, just like your circle of friends. By understanding what you're investing in, you'll make smarter choices and feel more confident in your portfolio.

Keeping up with news, trends, and financial education can feel overwhelming, but think of it as gossip for your finances. Stay informed about the latest market trends and investment opportunities without drowning in information. Subscribe to a few reliable financial newsletters and follow your company's bite-sized updates. Staying in the loop helps you make informed decisions and spot opportunities early.

Let's face it, everyone makes mistakes – even the best investors. The key is to turn those investment mishaps into valuable lessons. Every "oops" is just a future "aha!" Embrace your errors, analyze what went wrong, and adjust your strategy accordingly. It's all part of the journey create a fantastic life of financial freedom. Who run the world? Girls with great investment strategies! Connect with other women investors to share insights, experiences, and advice. Join investment clubs, attend financial workshops, or participate in online forums. Networking with like-minded women can provide support, inspiration, and valuable knowledge. Plus, it's a fun way to stay motivated and confident in your investment journey.

Chapter 13

Wrap-Up: Your Financial Dance-Off

Throughout this journey of financial enlightenment, we've explored pivotal strategies that can turn dreams into reality. From mastering the art of budgeting like a seasoned professional to decoding the mystique of investments, you've equipped yourself with the tools to make informed decisions. We've delved into the importance of diversification, ensuring your portfolio remains as vibrant and resilient as you are. And let's not forget the power of prudently managing debt, allowing you to free up resources to invest in your future.

In addition to these financial fundamentals, understanding and analyzing key metrics has positioned you on the front lines of wealth-building. We've embraced the importance of reviewing financial statements with as much excitement as binge-watching our favorite series, recognizing that long-term growth and consistency are key. You're now equipped with the knowledge needed to identify opportunities and make moves that reflect both caution and confidence. Here's to celebrating the highlights of your financial journey and being ready to embrace the future with optimism and vigor!

As you stand on the cusp of your financial journey, ready to take the stage and rock your wealth-building show, remember that every grand performance begins with a single step. Embrace the knowledge you've amassed, trust in your judgment, and don't shy away from taking calculated risks. Surround yourself with a supportive network, continue to educate yourself, and always stay curious. Your financial goals are within reach — it's time to channel your inner powerhouse, seize opportunities, and sculpt the prosperous future you deserve.

Feeling a bit nervous about diving into the real stock market? No worries! If you're not 100% ready, you can start by playing with real-time stock market apps.

These apps simulate the market and let you practice trading without any risk. It's like training wheels for your financial bike. But remember, the real magic happens when you take the leap into actual investing. There are no perfect conditions to begin; the perfect time to start is now. Besides, the thrill of seeing your real investments grow and being financially free is unmatched!
I hope you find as much value in this work as I put into it. This is my personal approach to investing, and while it worked for me, it's important to remember that it's not financial advice. Not every strategy may be the right fit for you, so I encourage you to take what resonates and adapt it to your own investing style. The stage is yours — step into the spotlight and let your success shine! I'm cheering you on and wishing you all the best.

Love,

Christina

Net Worth Overview

Date ___________________

Assets

Liquid Assets	Market Value
Checking Account	
Savings Account	
Cash	
Other:	
Investment Assets	
Retirement Account	
Stocks/Bond Inv.	
CDs	
Fixed Income	
Other:	
Personal Assets	
Personal Property	
Vehicles	
Collectibles	
Jewelry	
Other:	
Real Estate	
Personal Residence	
Rental Properties	
Other:	
Other Assets	
Life Ins. Cash Value	
Other:	
Business Interests	
Ownership Stakes	
Other:	
Total Assets	

Liabilities

Short-Term Liabilities	Market Value
Credit Card Debt	
Personal Loans	
Taxes Owed	
Other:	
Long-Term Liabilities	
Mortgage	
Student Loans	
Auto Loans	
Other:	
Total Liabilities	

Net Worth

Total Assets	
Total Liabilities	
Total Net Worth	

Notes

Budget Planner

Date _______________________

Total Income	Total Expenses	Ending Balance

Income	Amount
Total Income	

Notes

Expenses	Amount
Housing	
Utilities	
Food	
Debt	
Medical	
Insurance	
Donations	
Savings	
Personal	
Total Expenses	

Notes

Notes

Notes

Notes

Notes

INDEX

Wall Street 23
Walmart Inc. (WMT) 37
Walt Disney Co 38, 51
World War II 23
Yield 25